Finding
Connection and Meaning
in the face of Motor Neuron Disease

Finding
Connection and Meaning
in the face of Motor Neuron Disease

Living in a diseased body and experiencing myself as a healthy human being.

UTE SCHLOSSMACHER

with Zambodhi Hill

Finding Connection and Meaning in the face of Motor Neuron Disease
© Copyright 2024 Zambodhi Hill

All rights reserved. No part of this publication may be reproduced, distributed or transmitted in any form or by any means, including photocopying, recording, or other electronic or mechanical methods, without the prior written permission of the publisher, except in the case of brief quotations embodied in critical reviews and certain other noncommercial uses permitted by copyright law.

ISBN: 979-8-89109-715-5 - paperback

ISBN: 979-8-89109-716-2 - ebook

Dedication

On behalf of my sister Ute, this book is dedicated to her beloved daughter Franziska.
In addition this book is also dedicated to all people who require respiratory assistance and are therefore unable to communicate.
Last but not least this book is dedicated to everyone who helps those individuals with their communication.

Table of Contents

Part I

Foreword 11

Writing a book with eye movements. 15

Introduction* 21

The course of my life 25

Additional chapter by Zambodhi 39

First Symptoms* 55

Breaking the News* 65

Christmas letter to family and friends. 71

Living and working with MND 77

The Competition of the Hedgehog and the Hare* 81

Work* 99

Voice and Feelings* 105

Anger and Grief 113

The Challenge of Communication* 115

Moving, Handling and Touch* 137

Touch* 143

Itch* 147

Living a fulfilled life with MND* 149

The benefits of the MND Society* 157

Putting the House in Order* 161

My experience with Meditation* 171

Review of the Year 2014* 173

Facing death* 179

Hospital*, coming home* and farewells* 187

Part II

Brief introduction to Part II by Zambodhi 197

Lianne, one of Ute's main carers, doing all-day shifts 199

Christina, one of Ute's main carers, doing all-day shifts 203

Callie, one of Ute's main day time carers 207

Marcus, a voice from the family 211

Interview with Denise, then manager of the care agency 213

Interview with Margaret, General Manager at Horsfall House Care and Nursing Home 225

Excerpt from the response to Ute's resignation from her work as a nurse at Horsfall House 233

Farmer Mark 235

Farmer Sam 239

Apprentice Vasilios 245

Maria 251

Excerpt from a MND case study about Ute 257

Ute's contribution to Awareness 258

Hospitalisation 258

Home 259

Looking back 261

Acknowledgements 265

Part I

This part of the book consists of the chapters Ute wrote for her book, selected related documents, added communications with friends and the community, complementing chapters written by Zambodhi and carefully chosen personal messages.

Foreword
by Zambodhi

My sister Ute (pronounced Ootah) asked me on her death bed to publish this book on her behalf. She left a folder with 10 designated documents on her computer, the chapters she had written with her eye movements for this book during the time when the only movement control left to her was that of her eyes. These chapters and additional documents that she wrote using her eye gaze equipment are marked with an asterisk *.

For several years I suggested to Ute to write a book about her experiences. She always replied "Why?" adding "Anyway, I haven't got the time". Sometimes she said "Maybe when I am completely paralysed and can't do anything else any more…" She was too busy living and enjoying working as long as she could.

Ute had her own method of writing. She took a focus with different aspects of her life. Instead of narrating chronologically she shared for example how her work life was affected by the illness, starting at the time of the first symptoms up to the time when she was writing about it. Explaining how her mobility was affected she would go back again starting from the first symptoms and so on. That chapter particularly reveals that Ute was a teacher at heart and in both her professions she had training responsibilities. In her work as a nurse she was the certified moving and handling trainer and on the farm she trained apprentices together with her colleagues. When the editors pointed out to me that her going forwards and back in the timeline could be confusing for readers, I thought about it long and hard. Ute did not write her chapters in a particular chronological order, she did not have enough time to make the decision on how to organise them, so that fell to me. Structuring this book into chronological order would have required taking nearly every chapter Ute wrote apart. Eventually I decided to leave the chapters as she told her story, hoping that the way I organised them will help readers to make sense of what Ute wanted to share. I thought it better to leave it as authentic as possible.

Subsequently I found other documents that I believe would help to create a fuller picture of this part of her life that she was writing about. One of them was titled 'The course of my life' and written in 2012, a year after her diagnosis. Although she did not point it out to me at the time, I can only think that she must have written it with her book in mind when she still could write by hand and computer without aid.

It was tough to find a balance in the communications left by her, as Ute needed to write about mistakes in her care in order to get help and assist carers with understanding her needs, and therefore there is a risk of overburdening readers with the challenges she was facing. She used to communicate when there was a problem and expressed gratitude and contentment when things went well but did not write at length about that.

I like to encourage readers to read this book to the last sentence - or if that is not for you - please go to 'Acknowledgements' and read the very last sentence. You will find Ute's take on her experience in a nutshell there.

She stated in her introduction that "others will contribute", a wish that was fulfilled a few years after her death, when I set out to complete her book in accordance with her wishes. The date in brackets by the chapters is the date when she started to work on the respective document. Ute worked on each chapter until she felt it was finished, except the last one (Facing death) which she could not quite complete, but which is included. My additions to her chapters are in *Italics* to help you to see where I added to her chapters. I have been guided in this process by the editors, who have been tremendously helpful.

I structured the book into two parts. The first part contains Ute's documents, with additions from myself to fill in the picture. The second part comprises the interviews I carried out and writings from others I received after Ute's death.

Writing a book with eye movements

I also felt it necessary to describe how she wrote with her eyes, as it would enable readers to appreciate what a monumental effort went into writing this book. Even more so when Ute was in hospital. In order to help with the context, I have added all square brackets ['example'] to clarify or to supply missing words. With this I am hoping to assist with making sense of and the flow of reading. I made all additions to Ute's book with the intention to help her voice reach out.

When she lost the ability to speak and move her hands, Ute had two means of communication left to her, both involving her eye movements. One was the word board (see picture below). This could be easily transported anywhere, and communication with its help required concentration and skilful observations by all involved.

She needed to look at the four corners first, to find her desired letter and had to hold her gaze there until the carer was sure which corner she was looking at. Then she needed to look at the large coloured dots around the middle opening of the word board. When the carer had identified the right colour, they could then find the matching letter. For example if she needed the letter A, she would look at the respective corner, then at the green-colour dot, and when the carer had got the colour right, they could see that the green letter in the previously identified corner was A. Two pieces of information needed for every letter of every word. There was a 'wrong start again' field to look at for Ute at the top but no 'word completed' or 'new word' sign, which created difficulties with long words.

For example when Ute wanted to spell 'household', we would think she had completed the word *house* and started writing down a new word beginning as 'hold'. When we were unable to make sense of what she wanted to say, all she could do about it was start the word again, hoping that at some point the reader would continue the spelling until the word was complete.

Only much later did we become creative with the word board, asking Ute to look away from it when she had finished a word. This was so simple to do, and it could have saved her many repeats if we had thought of it earlier. The word board was made of heavy plastic and difficult to hold up for longer periods of time. It needed careful observation of the direction of Ute's eyes, especially with the coloured dots. In dull lighting (at night) it was even more difficult. It took so much concentration for Ute and her 'reader/s' and became harder towards the end of her life. Then we started to work with two people when she used it. One person concentrated on identifying the correct corner and colour, passing on the letter to the other person, who wrote down each identified letter, trying to make sense of words and sentences.

Another noteworthy learning point was about the added challenge that not all carers were fluent in English. Ute was sometimes stuck with someone not understanding a specific word, significant in order to carry out her care safely. Her daughter Franziska suggested looking the word up on people's phones and translating it online into their respective mother tongues. That was so simple and from then on saved Ute more suffering and anxiety.

The other form of communication for her was the 'eye-gaze equipment', basically a camera attached to the bottom of a computer screen that was connected to her laptop. The camera had to be calibrated to Ute's eye movements by her carers before she could use it. With the software installed she could write by looking at a virtual keyboard on the big screen. She held her gaze on the selected letter, which triggered a circle forming around that letter. When the circle was complete, the letter was clicked and appeared on the writing section of her screen.

In the first picture below, you can see the blue square with a white circle around the letter S (although the S is not visible as my camera could not reproduce the light conditions correctly). This was a result of Ute having looked at this letter long enough for the white circle to be nearly complete, which would next make the S appear in the upper writing part of the screen. When finished she could hold her gaze on the speech button for her writing to be read out.

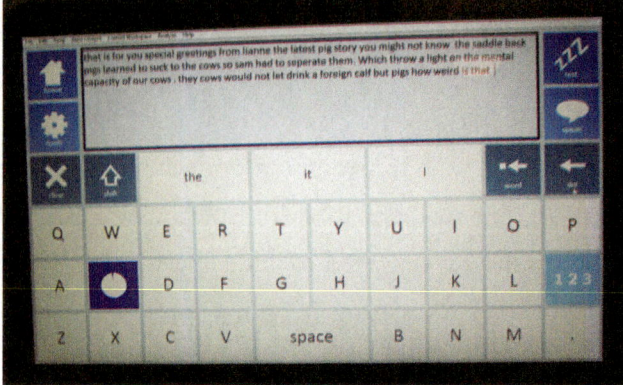

Writing a book with eye movements

Above, Ute in front of eye gaze screen, in the window sill is the connected laptop with the software

All the chapters Ute wrote directly for this book in the last few months of her life have been written with the eye-gaze equipment. The camera is so sensitive that it also wrote letters at times without Ute sitting there looking at it. It could be triggered by changes of the light in the room, or by movements such as a person passing or the wind moving the curtains. It could also give Ute the wrong letters at times, usually when the system needed re-calibrating. Calibrating her eye-gaze system was a skill that a core group of her day-time carers were trained in, to help her access this way of communication.

When Ute was in hospital, it became more complicated for her to write because the BiPAP mask (assisting her breathing) reached near her eyes, which confused the camera. Therefore, calibrating became much more difficult, many wrong letters came up, and she had to repeat some of them several times before it was correct.

Writing this book was so important to Ute that she managed to do it, despite these challenges. Moreover, she turned back from the threshold of death in order to write the last chapter ('Facing Death'), at the end of Part I.

Thank you for reading it.

Zambodhi

Introduction*
[29th October 2014]

This book is about living a healthy life with a condition called Motor Neuron Disease or short MND[1]. I will explore the physical, emotional, social and spiritual impact it has had on me, my friends, family, carers and professionals.

I share my experiences of living with MND with the group of people supporting me. I have been encouraged to write a book about it, because the people I shared with felt inspired by my experiences. I was reluctant to do so. There are enough books on the topic out there.

I changed my mind when I realised that I am part of a bigger picture. Not a bad fate has struck me - in fact, the contrary is the case. I play an active role living with my disease and not just that; I am part of a group of people who have chosen to walk this path together with me. Each of us has taken on a certain aspect of it. Mine is to gain and share

---
1   **MND** – Motor Neuron Disease also known as ALS. Motor neuron disease is one of a small group of neurological disorders that selectively affect motor neurons, the cells that control voluntary muscle activity including speaking, walking, swallowing, and general movement of the body. They are generally progressive in nature, and cause increasing disability and, eventually, death.

experiences of living with MND. I know this sounds a bit odd; it comes out of my growing perception of the spiritual aspects of my life.

Some years ago I had only a common perception of the world I live in. At that time any spiritual dimension of life was simply not relevant [for me] so I didn't even think about it. This very subtly changed as life happened. Now I recognise the spiritual aspects of my life because I perceive them to be just as real as I perceive the material world. This will be part of this book. The reader who does not have a spiritual perception may struggle here because without having a personal experience this appears to be a matter of belief.

You can take it as my way of making sense of my condition, or as a hypothesis which may or may not be proven by facts. I did the latter, years ago when I was confronted the first time with that type of experience. Having this hypothesis as an open question in the back of my mind I made my observation of daily life. I found that allowing the possibility of other dimensions than I would normally recognise deepened my perception. Out of that deepened perception I can see not only the losses in my life but also what they helped me to gain. Because I can focus on the gains instead of the losses, I perceive myself as a perfectly healthy person, living with a condition that gradually destroys my physical body. It needs a strong, healthy person to be able to deal with such a challenge.

I will not write this [book] on my own. That would be very one-sided because I know only one aspect of the whole

Introduction*

picture, that of my personal experiences. Together with other people's contributions, there will be a better chance to achieve more objectivity.

The supporting group includes friends, family and carers, who are committed to do things for me - the range goes from giving medication once a week, to doing cooking, cleaning, and gardening, to keeping contact with the doctor, to doing shopping or attending study groups. Physically I can't do a thing; everything has to be done for me. With the exception of personal care provision, all of this happens fully on a voluntary basis provided by family and friends.

The course of my life
[written in 2012, the year after Ute was diagnosed]

I was born on October 15, 1958 in Holzminden, Germany, my mother's hometown. My mother worked in a children's residential Home in Holthausen near Düsseldorf; my father did a preliminary internship for his social worker training. Six months after my birth, my mother found work in Bad Segeberg in a home for children from dysfunctional families and therefore my parents had a weekend marriage for some time. Nevertheless my sister was born in 1960 and my brother in 1961. Because my mother worked full time, I was looked after by a nanny along with other employees' children. That led to me addressing my mother as Frau Schlossmacher and „Sie" [A grammatical form in German to address people respectfully that one is not closely related to]. When my brother was about to be born, my sister was given into the care of our grandmother in Holzminden for one year.

After my father finished his apprenticeship, we lived in Gronau in Westphalia for eight months and moved in 1964 to Nikolausberg near Göttingen. My father worked as a social worker and later on as a probation officer, my mother gave up her job to look after the three of us. Unfortunately, my mother suffered from isolation and a lack of social recognition. I was four years old when we moved to Nikolausberg. By that time I had already been in hospital three times: once with a kidney infection, then appendix surgery and finally a tonsillectomy. The latter was done under local anaesthetic and is my earliest childhood memory. The circumstances of all three hospital stays were such that my parents were either unable [not allowed] to visit me at all or only to a very limited extent.

The hospital stays, my mother's full time work until I was three and my father's absence due to geographical distance set the scene for the theme in the first part of my early childhood: being abandoned. Looking back, I would say: I lived in fear of being abandoned or rejected. In order not to let these situations [feelings] arise, I proactively defended myself and hurt others before they could hurt me. I misunderstood criticism as rejection.

This belief was solidified when I was around ten years old. I wanted to go on a school trip; they had planned a hike followed by a bonfire. I had to stay in Kassel to take part and my father wouldn't allow it. I was desperate because all the other commuting pupils were also staying with friends. I ran into the broom closet, howling in anger and desperation. When my father came after me, I attacked him with the floor broom. My parents benevolently called me "the kid with the berserker[2] mind."

My memory of my early childhood years is obscure, probably based more on the stories of others and on photos than on real memories. I started school in 1964 having behavioural problems, which I don't remember. I had enuresis nocturna and apparently also defecated and received psychological care and support. What I remember is my fear of showing my school exercise books to my parents for them to sign, as I feared their 'moral sermons' because of my grades.

In 1967 we moved to Göttingen. From that time on I have clear memories. I attended the local elementary school. After the fourth grade, I could not enrol at the modern language high school because I wasn't doing well enough. The alternative would have been a girls' high school. In this situation, the director of my elementary school suggested sending me to a Waldorf [Steiner] school and put my parents in contact with other 'Waldorf parents' in Göttingen. I went to the nearest one, which was in Kassel, an hour's drive down the motorway from Göttingen. My two siblings followed a year later. Life as a commuting student began with a minimum of two hours travelling time every day, six days a week. It meant that my social contacts outside of school were somewhat limited. That became a problem during puberty because I couldn't go out in the evening with the others; my last train

---

2   Berserker
In the Old Norse written corpus, berserker were those who were said to have fought in a trance-like fury, a characteristic which later gave rise to the modern English word berserk. Berserkers are attested to in numerous Old Norse sources.

left at 9 o'clock in the evening. My school days were happy times until I passed my Abitur [equivalent of A levels].

I was a child with many interests. When my interest was piqued in any subject, I began to do my own research in order to understand more about it. An interest could develop from vacation experiences, a school trip (I found my love of geology while on a school trip), or something that provoked my dissent, like a high school question about whether Atlantis had really existed.

My parents had an increasingly difficult marriage over the years, with frequent arguments made worse by my father's uncontrolled outbursts of anger, or only barely controlled anger. This led to a domestic atmosphere of fear and thick air in which we children dared not grumble. As the eldest, I mediated many disputes between my parents. I was so embarrassed about these difficulties at home that I did not talk to anyone about it. That drove me into an inner isolation, I always experienced myself as standing next to myself, observing from the outside. Physically I was tense, especially in the shoulder girdle. I must have seemed very grumpy to those around me, while I felt normal – apart from standing beside myself.

I was seventeen years old when my siblings and I went on a five-week bike tour through Holland, Belgium, Luxembourg and Germany during the summer holidays. During this time, I panicked as soon as something did not go according to plan or problems arose. My siblings thoroughly experienced me and my panic and made me aware that I could respond differently to challenges. They stated, "You are like our mother" and commented on how miserable my self-inflicted stress was making me feel. We had tough discussions because they were not willing to tolerate my stress induced behaviour [any longer]. I attempted to change, since I finally realised how I was treating them and other people when I felt stressed. After our return I found that everyone had become nicer, including some people I really had not liked [before]. I was more relaxed, even in my body posture, and I made new friends.

My parents rented an apartment in Kassel so that the three of us could actually move out from our family home in Göttingen. They had realised that there was no other way for us to get through the increased afternoon attendance hours in the upper school, as the journey back would have been so much more time consuming, involving tram, train and local buses and taking two hours one way.

Our parents split up when I was eighteen and in the twelfth grade. I went to a psychologist because I suffered from the fact that both mother and father tried to get me on their side. After two sessions I realised that the psychologist could not help me and that I had to do the work on myself. My siblings were helpful as always, my sister not accepting the slightest trace of self-pity. So I had to find ways to overcome that. I memorised songs and sang until my mood improved. During this time I had several kidney infections that were treated with antibiotics.

After school I had enough of heavy studying. Although I always wanted to study archaeology, I decided to go into biodynamic agriculture[3]. Since there were no vacant apprenticeships [in Germany], I went to Carinthia [Austria] and began an apprenticeship in rural housekeeping on a biodynamic farm. After two years in housekeeping I ended up in a cowshed and discovered my passion for milking. These were happy years. I met my husband, we married and had a daughter. After my maternity leave [1983], I never had a paid job in agriculture again[4], although I always worked on the respective farms.

With the marriage there came a change that I didn't notice myself. My interests narrowed solely to farming, which was the interest I shared with my husband. I did not have any friends either, other than the ones my husband and I shared. Some of my previous friends withdrew. I gave up my own professional career for the sake of my husband's. After a short interlude in Germany, we worked in Luxembourg on a large biodynamic farm. Shortly before we went to Luxembourg, I had to have my left kidney removed. It was no longer functional after years of near-constant urinary-tract infections. The urinary tract-infections were a consequence of an unrecognised congenital kinked left ureter.

---

3   Biodynamics [BiodynamicAgriculture] is a holistic, ecological, and ethical approach to farming, gardening, food, and nutrition https://www.biodynamics.com/what-is-biodynamics

4   [until she moved to England in 2006 and started to do paid work on the farm here.]

In 1989 we moved to the Belgian Eiffel and, together with another family, converted a farm to biodynamic farming. It was years of hard work, but I always enjoyed doing it. While working, I didn't realise that I was not aware of my own needs. Nor did I notice how life slowly drained from our marriage. I was completely shocked when, a few days after my thirty seventh birthday [1995] and after 14 years of living together, my husband terminated our marriage and explained that he now wanted to live with the woman in our partner family. This blew up both families with a great bang and great pain for both children and adults.

For me, that was the turning point in my life. It was immediately clear to me that I couldn't win the old relationship back, even though I would have given anything for it. While I felt the enormous loss acutely, I directed my awareness towards new insights and learning that came out of this situation into my life. I opted to move forward with whatever insights I could gain.

This process coincided with my waking up to the spiritual side of being. I changed a little more every day. Those around me thought I looked good and much younger, even though I cried regularly while milking. I got to know the people around me in new ways, nurtured close friendships, went to the church choir and revived my diverse interests. Suddenly, in our farm shop, I was told by customers about their deepest experiences. Over time, they also told me that they used to be afraid of me because I had always seemed so grim.

I made my first conscious spiritual experiences when I learned that chakras are real because I could suddenly feel my heart chakra. I completely changed my inner alignment within a few weeks. I suddenly could not eat meat any more, although I still liked it - but I could no longer digest it. I haven't had any alcohol since the breakup. Not in the acute situation because I knew I couldn't tolerate alcohol, but because I didn't like the effects of alcohol on my body. Even today, I rarely eat meat, mostly in winter and only biologically dynamically produced. Now I am avoiding it again because it instantly tires me.

I stayed on our farm in Belgium for two more years, even though the families had broken apart. I would have liked to continue farming there if all other adults had done what they said they would do - to leave the farm - but nothing happened. [Ute would have been happy to work with new colleagues] When all of them still worked on the farm two years later, I left. Our daughter was fifteen at the time and wanted to continue going to school in Belgium. Therefore I decided to stay in the town of St. Vith and look for a new job.

First, I became a recipient of social benefits. I could not register as job seeking because I never had a paid job even though I had pulled my weight working fully on the farms all those years. My Austrian professional training was not recognised in Belgium and I was really starting at zero.

I then attended nursing school and graduated as a nurse after three years. During this time my daughter ran away from home, dropped out of school and didn't want to have anything to do with me any more. My attempts to reach her failed. The only thing I could do was to let her go completely and trust her unconditionally. That was certainly the greatest lesson I learned in my life. I overcame this challenge with the help of prayer and trust that there is a deeper wisdom behind the visible events. Within a few years I had to give up the three parts of my life that I loved most: first my marriage, then my beloved job, then my own child.

I then worked for a few years as a district nurse for a nursing service in Luxembourg and was quickly entrusted with the difficult cases and with palliative[5] care. However, there was bullying going on within the nursing service, so I resigned as soon as my turn came. In 2006 I took a sabbatical. I had a strong inner conviction that I had to go to England because the people I wanted to work with would be there. I didn't know any of these people yet, except my sister Zambodhi.

I moved in with my sister in Stroud in July 2006 in a tiny one-bedroom flat where we still live together to this day [2012, a year before we left the flat]. We had the idea, together with a group of local people, to set up a bespoke service in the local community for people living with life-limiting and terminal illness. But I found that I did not understand the English culture enough yet nor the conditions under which people work in England. So I decided to get to know my new country and its people better and looked for work in nursing.

---

5   Palliative care is an interdisciplinary medical caregiving approach aimed at optimising quality of life and mitigating suffering among people with serious, complex, and often terminal illnesses.

I found it in a local nursing home that specialises in dementia care. I also became a member of the local biodynamic farm and started working there one day a week. At the time of writing I work two days in the nursing home and two and a half days on the farm.

Preparing salad packs in the shed for farm customers

In my nursing work I was again confronted with bullying after my first year of working there. I was not the only one being bullied, some of my colleagues were also affected. I was suspended from work and had to contact the union to clarify how to deal with all the allegations against me. This time I did not quit, but continued to do my work and openly showed why I did or did not do certain things in my nursing work. It was not easy in a climate full of open mistrust. Eventually the management of the care home changed and I can now contribute my potential to a team that works well together with the new management.

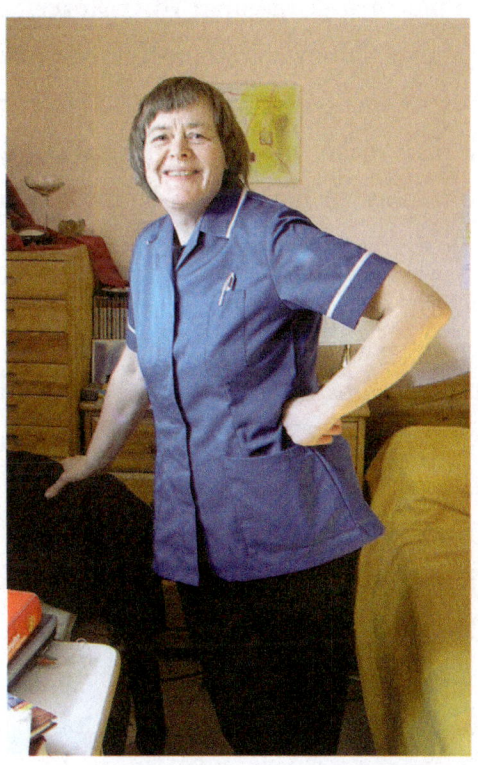

Ready to go to work in the nursing home

In addition to my work, I pursue my diverse interests. I have an interest in observing nature, which over the years has led to questions about how the forces of life can be perceived and how I can train my own organs of perception for this accordingly. Then there is my lifelong interest in the stars. Pure observation of the heavens has now become the question of the relationship between the human being on the earth and the world of the stars. I have joined the work on both respective topics in local study groups near me. Another interest is inner training and meditation. In addition, I work as a tutor in biodynamic training. My approach is to observe inner and outer activity and to come from these observations to reliable experiences. One day a week I work with young people who have been through challenges in their journey through education. In my sessions I provide practical and observational exercises and themes around biodynamic agricultural issues. I started this job in January [2012], knowing that one day I will no longer be able to work physically because of my diagnosis and associated health problems.

For two years I had been observing progressive muscle atrophy in my right leg and the onset of signs of paralysis in my right foot. Now, a year after my MND diagnosis, my right foot is paralysed and my left foot shows signs of paralysis. I wear splints on both legs so I can still walk. My strength in legs and lower torso has significantly decreased. I can only walk short distances, using two sticks to get around on uneven terrain and have difficulty climbing stairs. My balance is bad, I have to control every movement with my eyes to keep my balance. My body feels heavy, every movement costs me effort and nothing works by itself any more. Despite this, I have always been able to adapt. So far, the disease has not stopped me from doing the things I want to do. Of course, there are many things I can no longer do, but there are still enough things that I can do. At the moment I am still working in my two professions, nursing and farming. But the day is approaching when I will give up all physical activity.

When I look at the course of my life, it could be argued that I have drawn a hard lot. Yet, I have never felt that way. I have felt rather happy most of my life and I still do to this day.

It is also clear to me that none other than myself is responsible for what happens to me in life. I see my illness in this context: it will probably give me the opportunity to experience something that I cannot experience in any other way, something which I wanted and have decided to learn.

> *Ute was sure that she had made such a choice before entering this lifetime. It made sense to her that she did exist before her conception and that she would continue to exist and develop after her death.*

Additional chapter by Zambodhi

In 1997, which was two years after her marriage broke up, having been a passionate biodynamic farmer for nearly twenty years, Ute left the farm and subsequently began her training as a nurse. Nursing, it turned out, was equally close to her heart, and once her training was completed in the beginning of the new millenium, she enjoyed working as a district nurse in Luxembourg, just a short distance away from her home in Belgium.

Already during her nursing training, she felt drawn to the field of palliative [symptom relief] care. Ute engaged with patients as well as their family members, realising that many people felt helpless when their loved ones or clients were approaching the end of their lives. While patients had been given adequate medical and nursing support, it was the art of communication and supporting the journey in other ways that seemed to be needed. Ute engaged wholeheartedly in this field, gently guiding family members through the change of communication, when everyday things became symbols for the process of the dying patient.

For example, once, the wife of a dying man greeted Ute at the door, deeply worried, saying her husband had asked her to bring him his driving licence, the house key and the car key. He wanted them right on his bedside table. His wife had responded by explaining to him that he could not possibly drive in his condition and that he did not need any of those things. He was upset that she did not bring him what he wanted, while she was heartbroken about his distress and full of fear that he would be at risk if he had access to his car keys. Ute sat down with her, explaining that it was most likely that her husband was feeling the changes in his condition and that he indeed was close to death. She elucidated the three required items as symbols rather than as something to be used physically. The keys to the house and car and the driving licence had been needed throughout his adult life when going out on a journey, and now he might sense that he may be leaving soon. In that moment these everyday items became symbols. This made sense to his wife and she could do what he had asked for without fear that he would attempt to get in the car (Ute had also pointed out that he was in fact much too weak to achieve that at his stage of the illness). Her husband was very pleased when she put everything on his bedside table and fell asleep. He died peacefully the next day.

A few years before Ute began to work as a nurse I had encountered terminal illness, through a close friend, Rosemary, being diagnosed with incurable cancer. Our friendship deepened very much until she died five years later. Rosemary was the first person where I was present at the moment of death. This experience transformed me. From then on I began to appreciate the simple things in life, for example the fact that I have the strength to do everything I need to do. Yet, I also learnt that, because I wanted to give support, I overlooked my own physical or emotional exhaustion and my need to deal with my grief over Rosemary's suffering. I found that my ambitions to help at times simply were beyond my physical and emotional capacity and learnt how important it is to look after my own needs. And then I made the same mistake again when Ute was ill. Was it a mistake? When I look back now I do not regret it, even though it took me a year to recover after Ute died.

In the early years of the new millennium, Ute and I had long conversations on the phone, talking through similar experiences in this field that she and I were challenged with, Ute with her nursing work in Luxembourg and me with my voluntary (at the local hospice) and therapy work (sound therapy) here in England. We helped each other to respond to these situations with as much openness and sensitivity as we could and contemplated questions, such as where people can find support in their local communities and how we could develop a sense of recognition when everyday items or rituals suddenly become symbols during an ongoing process.

During this time, together with a friend and colleague, I used to run workshops on the theme of death and dying. These workshops were about listening, caring and communication, inspired by our work with Anthroposophy[6] and our training as art and movement therapists respectively. Marshall Rosenberg's Nonviolent Communication[7] and Elisabeth Kübler-Ross'[8] work about death and dying further informed many practical aspects of our work. We were using art, movement and music with sounding bowls[9] to enhance deep listening, connect with the heart and help people to feel centred in themselves. We also became involved with accompanying terminally ill people with sounding bowl music in hospitals, care homes or their own homes for some years.

In 2006, Ute moved from Belgium to England at the age of 47. By this time I had already lived in this country for 13 years. Our phone conversations between 2001 and 2005 [Ute in Belgium and me in England] and her wish for a new beginning, led to the plan for Ute to move to Stroud in order for us to work together. Ute joined my friend and me with the workshops and she became involved with the initiative to bring music to the dying before she found her work on the farm and in the local care home.

---

6   [from Greek Anthropos - the human being and Sophia - wisdom, - 'wisdom of the human being'] - founded by Dr Rudolf Steiner in 1912, an Austrian philosopher, scientist and artist, who postulated the existence of a spiritual world comprehensible to pure thought and fully accessible only to the faculties of knowledge latent in all humans.

7   Nonviolent Communication (NVC) is a process of communication created by psychologist Dr Marshall Rosenberg. It is a compilation of ideas about compassionate human behaviour, packaged to meet the needs of modern times.

8   Elisabeth Kübler-Ross was a Swiss-American psychiatrist, a pioneer in near-death studies, and author of the internationally best-selling book, On Death and Dying, where she first discussed her theory of the five stages of grief, also known as the "Kübler-Ross model"

9   https://soundingbowlwork.wordpress.com/

Another group formed in 2007, which Ute and I were part of, with the aim to create support for people affected by terminal illness in the community, ideally with access at the point of need and also free of charge. This was both with regards to practical, social and non-religious pastoral needs. At our regular meetings, we engaged with a holistic vision of a large farm with extra supported living space, where people could come to live for a while or – if they chose to – until they died. We thought it would be helpful for people facing their own death to experience the cycle of the year in and with nature. The centre of the farm would be a warm kitchen with an Aga[10]. The idea was that anybody seeking company would be able to have a hot drink, meal or a snack round the kitchen table, and farmers could warm up when the weather might be rough. Living quarters would offer calm and peace to withdraw to.

Much more thought and detail than I can do justice to here went into it, but after two years we still could see no way to fund it and since none of us had the means of doing so, nor the enthusiasm and skill to engage with fundraising, we let go of the initiative. Around this time, in 2009 after Ute had been living and working in England for three years, the first symptoms of her illness began to be noticeable but not yet identifiable as symptoms of an illness. After another year or so it was clear that something was wrong. And that

---

10 Aga is a brand of cast-iron stored-heat cooking stove

Finding Connection and Fulfillment in the Face of Motor Neuron Disease

it was serious. In the Summer of 2011 came the diagnosis of MND/ALS[11].

This is where her book begins.

When Ute moved to England in 2006 there was nowhere she could live other than with me. Without work, she could not rent a flat and without an address she could not apply for work. So she moved into the flat I was renting until she would find something later on – or so we thought. Ute had the tiny bedroom to herself and I slept on the sofa in the living/sitting/through room, which also had a kitchen corner. Somehow it worked when Ute had sown a curtain, dividing off the sofa and side table from the 'walk through' bit to the bathroom and Ute's bedroom and of course the kitchen. When I drew the curtain round my 'bed' at night, at least I had a bedroom for the time being. And Ute had access to the kitchen and to the staircase for the front door without entering my sleeping quarters. Ute and I always thought that we had accomplished something amazing by sharing a one-bedroom flat and still feeling the friendship and sisterhood that connected us. We got used to the incredibly narrow space and managed most challenges with humour. We used to joke about things falling down when piles of paper had grown too high, thanking gravity for them not falling upwards towards the ceiling, which would have been too high for either of us to pick them up from there. Both of us enjoyed being

---

11   ALS - Amyotrophic Lateral Sclerosis (Another name for MND, used in other countries)

Additional chapter by Zambodhi

outdoors and the large garden at the college and the bit of garden behind the house compensated for the small flat.

When Ute's symptoms began to be noticeable we could still maintain 'normal life' for another year or so but the time came, when Ute's illness began to challenge and change our sister relationship. One of the biggest challenges came when we could no longer live together. Our flat had a staircase of some 15 steps on which no stairlift could be mounted. In the beginning of 2013 it was clearly only a matter of time when Ute would no longer be able to get up those stairs. In the previous year we had talked about this and I took up suggestions from friends to look at possible dwelling places for us, when they came up for renting. Ute was against this because she held on to the belief that something would come up, which would allow her to stay on the farm. Hawkwood College, where we rented our flat, leased land to the farm and that was where part of Ute's farm work took place. On one occasion Ute came with me looking at a bungalow available to rent in the local area. The visit resulted in Ute spending the evening crying in her bedroom and me feeling miserable about having persuaded her to come and take a look. I realised that I could not resolve this on my own, I would have to go at Ute's pace, even though the need for a new home might become an emergency situation – which it duly did.

In July 2013, when we returned from our last trip to Ute's friends in Belgium and Luxembourg, I helped Ute up the stairs again. I realised that I could no longer carry on doing that. I had to lift up each leg, move it up one step and then lift the other, whilst Ute could barely hang on to the bannister, trying to pull herself upwards. (video link to one of the last occasions she made it upstairs with the help of a friend, just before she had to move out. https://youtu.be/a7ZPeStTayY

My back was giving me a lot of pain because I had to bend so low whilst taking the weight of Ute's paralysed legs. It needed doing twice for each step. I did not have the courage to share this with Ute, but I realised that I was too exhausted and in too much pain to do this one more time. The recent intensive physical efforts when travelling with her had taken it out of me.

I went outside, took my mobile phone with me and phoned Sam, the farmer, explaining that an emergency had arisen because I could no longer cope with helping Ute up the stairs. Sam was very understanding. Earlier in the year Ute and I had visited his family admiring their new home in Brookthorpe, where the farm leased part of their land. Sam's large bungalow with so many rooms that one of them was 'spare' looked great and without saying much the question whether Ute might be able to live here one day hung in the air. After my call Sam talked it over with his wife and they offered Ute to stay with them over the Summer. His wife and the children were planning to visit family abroad for a month and during this time another solution could hopefully be found. When Sam called back Ute answered the phone. I had asked him not to tell her that I had called him. When Ute hung up she turned to me beaming and said "You see, something has come up when I needed it. Sam just called and offered me to move into their spare room from tomorrow. He'll be here in the morning to help with the move. No need for you to worry so much." I said nothing but drew a quiet sigh of immense relief.

It was clear that this was only a temporary solution and Ute still needed to find another home because the family of four could not absorb someone into their home with increasingly severe disability, who would soon need even more space for carers being present night and day.

Another decision was coming up for us and I realised it had to be Ute's. She decided that she no longer wanted to share future accommodation with me because she did not want me to experience her expected deterioration at such close hand on my own. She would have agreed for us to live together again, if we had been able to live with a small community with one or two more people in our next home. This was a painful moment for both of us. We had been together all this time and now as she became so ill, Ute chose to go it alone. With her professional background in palliative care she was only too aware how relatives could suffer from witnessing deterioration without being able to do anything about it. I felt inwardly stretched and drawn. I needed to find my own home and I knew I would need to spend a lot of my time in Ute's next home to help as best I could.

Doing practical things for Ute caused lots of frustration for her because she repeatedly found that her requests had not been carried out to the letter. I guess Ute poured out her frustrations to me because we knew each other so well. While it was very challenging for me to experience her dissatisfaction, I needed to step back inwardly and develop a sense of being bestowed with a direct view into Ute's inner reality and the privilege of being allowed that. Soon I realised that I was not alone – others close to her, especially those of her carers who spent all day with her and whom she trusted deeply, also received what I was calling the 'tough stuff'.

Ute's health began to deteriorate more rapidly, just as she had moved into her last home, a rented bungalow with four bedrooms on the other farm site, next door to farmer Sam. Her manual wheelchair needed to be replaced by an electric one, she soon after needed a head support mounted on it, when her neck muscles became too weak to hold her head up. Eating became increasingly dangerous for her until she gave up and moved on to tube feeding in August 2014.

From the end of 2013, I underwent a process of gradual realisation that our life-long deep connection as sisters and close friends was changing profoundly. I witnessed how Ute was completely occupied in the battlefield of her many losses of skills in the first eight months of 2014. During that time it was difficult to get anything right for her at all. And humour, essential for us while we were sharing the flat, got lost somewhere along the way. With the loss of her ability to speak and to move her hands, communication had many moments of desperation for Ute with me and others. She would end up crying when she could not make herself understood and I would feel guilty about not understanding what she wanted.

A terrible dynamic... This happened before Ute had the eye-gaze computer equipment. Shortly after she received it she wrote to me: "if you want to help me, make me laugh." A real challenge for me at first, because I felt devastated about her suffering.

Ute and I had done so much together, knowing each our strengths and weaknesses. We used our strengths and each of us contributed with what we could do best. We used to refer to that jokingly as 'your department'. For example Ute did the cooking, 'my department' was shopping and washing up. Another example is that I booked any travelling arrangements, whereas Ute collected information about the destination and explored what we might want to do. If any further bookings were needed, she handed it back to me. I could ask Ute for almost any information I wanted. She was so widely read and informed that I often followed her answers with another question "How do you know that?" Then she would tell me where she had read it or how she had come across the information. Only very rarely would she say that she had forgotten where she got the information.

Although I did not see Ute every day (but still several times every week) in the first few months of us being in different living quarters, it was as though I walked by her side all the way, through the stormy and rocky times and the calm ones. As Ute got more and more disabled she became more demanding in my eyes. I lived a 25 minutes drive away from her home and worked whilst also studying for a Master's degree. Many days needed careful timing to fit in her shopping, preparing her medications when it fell to me to do it all and organising other things around her household apart from being involved in communications when things had gone wrong. On one occasion when I had given up my dinner time in order to bring Ute what she needed, she started to cry when she saw me coming into the kitchen, where she was tube fed by her carers. She could not speak without speaking aid and seemed terribly upset about me being there. Her carer explained that I had arrived at the wrong time for Ute. I was already stressed about fitting everything into my day and upset about the implied expectation that I would have known from a distance how Ute's day had turned out timing-wise. I thought she was very demanding towards me and was frustrated that whatever effort I made did not seem to be good enough or to count at all. I was so disappointed that our sister relationship had lost its mutuality and that there seemed never to be a thank-you, just some satisfaction when I happened to get something right for her. This feels harsh to write but it was my reality for some time. Then it changed again to Ute expressing appreciation and care, once she was more settled as she had become completely paralysed.

Only when I consciously had said 'goodbye' to the sister relationship as I had known it, could I let Ute be free in my mind to make her way the best she could through the rough patches, while concentrating on how I could support her better with practical things she asked for. My waking up or turning point came on one occasion when Stefan, our brother, visited us and he and I went to buy materials to

Additional chapter by Zambodhi

make a desk for Ute, high enough that the electric wheelchair would fit underneath. We used a good deal of the day to get everything together. Ute had asked for a set of sockets to be attached to the desk allowing four plugs to go in for her electrical equipment. Stefan and I found one such socket set allowing for eight plugs and were very happy that this would be even better, anticipating that more electrical equipment would be needed. However, when we came back, Ute was really upset that we had made our own decision to buy eight instead of the four sockets that she had asked for. I was exhausted, frustrated and disappointed that she didn't even thank us for spending most of the day helping her with this, especially Stefan, who then went on to work turning the boards into a bespoke desk. Before she was so ill, Ute would have thought about the time that people gave her and expressed care about their efforts to support her.

While I was mourning the sister I no longer had, I could not see that I needed to change my attitude and let go of the past. I found that I needed to understand my own feelings and needs before I could understand Ute's. I needed empathy for having spent a day in different DIY shops, whilst I was desperate for a rest myself. Through reflecting on my own unmet need for recovery and my wish for recognition for the efforts of that day, I finally became peaceful within myself, my awareness became free to focus away from myself and suddenly I saw the bigger picture: Ute in the midst of a battle with loss of self-determination and control, fighting fiercely for every little bit of independence. Because everything practical in her life was dependent on others, she was so desperate about her instructions being carried out to the letter – that was one way she could still control what happened. My sister who had been one of my closest friends and collaborators, which intensified for me since she had moved to England, was at this point occupied with fighting for her remaining independence and survival. In the light of this battle my disappointment about loss of mutuality in our sisterhood and friendship paled into insignificance. I could no longer expect Ute to understand me – I needed to understand her.

I succumbed to my conclusion that it would likely be a one-sided relationship and I found quite soon that I was completely wrong. I reminded myself not to feel attached to Ute's responses to what I did for her, but instead viewed critical feedback from her as part of the journey she was on rather than my personal failure in supporting her. Astonishingly, things began to improve quickly and humour was finally making a re-entry. We began to have good laughs about funny things that happened on the farm and other things we both found amusing. Ute wrote down amusing events and contributed with beginnings of quotes which we knew well and shared just for fun.

When Ute became completely paralysed she seemed to be even more at ease and humour, jokes and her seeing the funny side of life appeared frequently on her screen. Below an example:

"This is for you [Ute writing this to me because I loved the pigs especially] the latest pig story: you might not know that the saddle back pigs learnt to suckle the cows, so Sam [the farmer] had to separate them. Which throws a light on the mental capacity of our cows. They would never let a foreign calf drink but they allowed the pigs [to help themselves]. How weird is that? Sam did not know whether that was embarrassing or not… [see this text in the screen photo above in 'Foreword']

Another subject of endless amusement for Ute was spiders in the house. Most of her carers and myself did not like spiders, whilst Ute had no problem with their presence. Every now and then she would write something like "Spider under the door handle of the bathroom door, or above your head on the ceiling" etc and then witness how her carers or guests and myself tried not to freak out with fear. After writing a warning on her screen, she laughed so hard that tears rolled down her cheeks when observing various people in the room trying to escape or to deal with it.

Ute focussed on her participation in meetings and study groups, all taking place in her home, on communication and on getting her book done. She then had a few great months, in spite of being completely paralysed, living with her level of disability and its challenges but also lots of blessings with her care. She got on with activities, enjoyed contact with people that mattered to her and laughed about the funny moments in life. During that time I felt our sister-relationship healing from all the bruises it had received in the previous stages of her illness. Whatever I had missed was restored and we could have conversations again as Ute had developed her eye writing to good speed. And finally, to use Ute's words, she 'got round to' writing her book.

The eye-gaze writing equipment was only one of several technologies that she relied on. Without the PEG[12] feeding tube for example, Ute, would not have had the time to write most of this book. In fact, the feeding tube, replacing treacherous and painfully slow meals, freed up many hours on a daily basis and prevented life threatening difficulties with swallowing food. It also gave her more time to live and write.

Working with the book now I still feel like team working it with her, as real as it can be. As the book gets published, I am looking forward to what will happen next. Like Ute, I hope and trust that this book will make its way into the world and into the hands and hearts of the people who can benefit from it.

---

12   PEG - feeding tube inserted directly into the stomach

First Symptoms*
[9th October 2014]

I used to be a physically active person. Most of my adult life I worked on biodynamic farms in various European countries. After my marriage broke up I did a three-year nurses' training in Belgium and then worked full time as district nurse in Luxembourg. I spent the evenings in my extensive garden until the light faded. The physical work in my garden balanced the demanding work in the district beautifully.

In 2006, I took a sabbatical and in July moved to England because I had the feeling that the people I wanted to work with would be there. Apart from my sister with whom I shared a one-bedroom flat for the next seven years, I did not yet know any of them.

My sister Zambodhi lived in a privately run adult-education facility, including land leased to a biodynamic farm. It is set up as Community Supported Agriculture. (Abbreviation:

CSA).[13] I was delighted to find a CSA on my doorstep, which was exactly what my husband and I had envisioned for our farm in Belgium, but failed to achieve due to the lack of interest in such a model locally. As soon as Zambodhi and I became members of this farm here, I started working there. In addition, I found a part-time job at a nursing home nearby. Although I have had to face some challenges in my nursing work, I was now experiencing the happiest time of my life. I extended my work on the farm to two and a half days a week because I loved farming so much and the work was needed. But I did not reduce my nursing work because I needed the income. I worked about 50 hours a week and felt very comfortable doing it. I loved going outside in the summer evenings until dusk to work in the carrot field or in the flower beds, just like I had done in my garden in Belgium before.

My sister was longing for a bit of private space because the college is quite busy in the summer. We chose a neglected slope behind our flat to be turned into a secluded garden. This work involved significant earth work; requiring spade, pickaxe and some tree felling. I happily started to work on that in Summer 2009.

The next year, in 2010 this work seemed to be much more physically exhausting than it had been. So did some

---

13   CSA, Community Supported Agriculture, a model that supports the farmers independently from the actual produce every week of the year. The shareholders receive varying amounts of vegetables depending on seasons and crops whilst the farmers can rely on their income. Shareholders can participate in farming tasks and festivals and other celebrations can take place in the farming community. Biodynamic meat is available to buy for those who want it.

First Symptoms*

of the farm work for example wheeling a full wheelbarrow uphill, which had never been a problem before. In October 2008 I had turned 50 so I was wondering whether my loss of physical strength was age related. In order to carry on with this type of heavy physical work I had to engage my will to overcome the feeling of exhaustion. I carried on but it was not easy going any more and I only managed by working less evening times on the farm.

When looking in the mirror I observed from time to time my eyes looking glossy as though I had a fever. I felt perfectly well; no cold, no infection whatsoever. I discussed it with my sister who had observed the same changes. This was rather strange, looking feverish and feeling well. Walking barefoot I stumbled over my right big toe that tended to drag across the ground. I thought I was a bit inattentive. In October 2008 I did some hiking in the countryside. Already then my right foot appeared a bit weak, I stumbled over uneven ground. I credited it to an old injury in my right knee.

In Summer 2010 I noticed in the evenings in bed some thick saliva in the back of my throat. Nothing to worry about because it didn't affect my wellbeing, but it was a kind of presence. In the Autumn it vanished but reappeared the next summer. Because I have a mild pollen allergy I thought this was part of the allergy.

One beautiful Sunday morning in 2010 I climbed a stepladder in my nighty at six am in order to disable a smoke sensor, which sounded an alarm due to low battery power. On this occasion Zambodhi noticed that my right leg was thinner than the left one. The only explanation I had at that time was the old knee injury, because apart from occasional stumbling I felt perfectly well.

The same summer we went to North Devon for holidays. Zambodhi went bodyboarding at Putsborough Sands and I set off for a good swim. Surprisingly my right leg could not withstand the force of the waves, I was not in control and in danger of being swept away by the water. I did not know what was going on but for the first time in my life I felt unsafe in the sea. I went out of the water feeling rather dizzy. I had just made it back to my belongings when I collapsed onto the sand. The sea, the people, the sky all turned into yellow and disappeared behind a veil of sounds. I was unable to move, my pulse was flying, my breathing shallow. I saw the lifeguard people about twenty metres away, realising that they would not be able to help me because I could not use my voice to call for help. I observed shock-like symptoms and decided to deal with them. I tried to control my breath, slowed it down and deepened it to get my pulse down, which had some effect after a while. When I felt a bit better I sat up but the symptoms returned straight away. So I lay back down again until I managed to sit up a fair bit later on.

This experience was deeply disturbing for two reasons: it felt life threatening and I found myself in the middle of a busy beach and close to the lifeguards, yet helpless and

First Symptoms*

seemingly entirely on my own.[14] The next few days I felt weak and unsafe. Emotionally I was deeply disturbed. I knew this was some kind of overreaction of my nervous system but I had no idea what made me react in this way. While I didn't know what it was, it was now perfectly clear *something* was wrong.

Because my right foot was getting weaker, I was twisting my ankle more and more often and falling without warning, I went to see an osteopath[15]. He examined me carefully, checked my reflexes and came to the conclusion that something in my spine was not working properly, which was affecting the motor nerves of my right leg between the S1 and S2 vertebrae [between the sacrum and coccyx]. After his treatment I felt better. I did not twist my ankle as often any more, but within a few months the weakness in my right big toe developed into 'drop foot' [weakness of foot muscles that make the toes hang down when walking, creating a high risk of catching the foot on things and stumbling]. I underwent further examinations; it was x-rayed then an MRI scan done and I went to various specialists all of whom concluded that

---

14 Ute waited until she recovered without alerting anyone when she had recovered enough to do so. I came out of the sea much later, when she was back on her feet. She told me about the event but did not want any other follow up as she could walk and do everything necessary.
15 Osteopathy is a system of diagnosis and treatment for a wide range of medical conditions. It works with the structure and function of the body and is based on the principle that the well-being of an individual depends on the skeleton, muscles, ligaments and connective tissues functioning smoothly together. https://www.osteopathy.org.uk/visiting-an-osteopath/about-osteopathy/

there was something wrong with the bones of my spine. This would need to be examined and treated by an orthopaedist[16].

Personally, I did not believe that for two reasons: the complete absence of pain and the fact that I had lived with my damaged spine all my life without motor problems [When Ute was a child she had a correction of the curvature of her spine. It was not perfect, but she could live with it without any pain or impairment of her mobility. It was not obvious to others]. I insisted on seeing the neurologist rather than an orthopaedic consultant. In the meantime I developed so-called fasciculations first in my right leg, later in both. Fasciculations are uncontrolled, trembling movements of muscles. At that time I had no idea what that was, but I noticed that this 'fluttering of muscles' always affected one or two segments of a spinal, motoric nerve. This told me that my symptoms were something neuro-muscular, a disease of the nerves rather than of the bones. The only disease I knew which would fit these criteria was MND. By the end of the year 2010 the fasciculations had extended into my lower and upper legs and lower back.

Around Christmas I experienced them one night in my throat. At Christmas time I went through a lot of frightening nights, observing my increasing symptoms carefully. At that time in particular I experienced a kind of constant background 'noise' in my body caused by the over stimulation of my motor nerves. Being confronted with these symptoms I

---

16   Orthopaedist: concerned with conditions involving the musculoskeletal system

First Symptoms*

came to the conclusion that I indeed was facing my worst-case scenario, which was having MND. Once I got that clear for myself, I felt a bit better again because at least I knew what I would have to face.

It took another six months before I got the official diagnosis. This did not bother me because personally I already had clarity about the situation and the official death sentence could wait until I felt stronger [within myself]. For that reason I didn't attempt to speed the investigation up.

I had to undergo a nerve-conduct test, a kind of torture in which electric currents are applied to certain muscles and the nerve activity is measured. Pathological nerve activity was found exactly in the same regions of muscles where I had my fasciculations. I saw the neurologist in May 2011. I sat on the examination bench with an undressed upper body, and he walked in and observed my back. I felt the moment when he realised what was going on. A moment later he said to his assistant: "I don't like this," and I knew what he meant: the fasciculations. He examined me and checked all my reflexes. I asked about my diagnosis. He didn't want to tell me and said it needs further investigation such as blood check, lumbar puncture, another nerve-conduct test. I asked what the worst-case scenario would be? As a good doctor he replied by asking me what *my* worst case scenario would be. I told him MND. He replied that at present he could not confirm, but he could also not exclude it either. We both knew what the diagnosis would be but he had to exclude all other possible causes first, one of which would be MS. I personally knew it was not MS because I did not experience tiredness; one of the key symptoms of MS. On the contrary I felt more energetic than ever before although my physical life became harder and harder.

In July 2011 I had another appointment with the neurologist after all the other tests were done. Zambodhi insisted on coming with me, so we went together. He came to call me into his office with the words: "You are the lady I was so worried about last time." And sure enough he delivered the diagnosis: Motor Neuron Disease. I wanted to know the prognosis. Again he was very diplomatic and pointed out Stephen Hawking was living with it for more than 40 years. Other people die within three months of being diagnosed. I would be somewhere in between.

The final diagnosis was a relief for me. I got what I expected. I could now tell everybody what I have and people would stop telling me I should see the orthopaedic consultant and undergo back surgery.

How it is for a consultant having to deliver a death sentence, I don't know. I was probably one of the more easy cases: no shock, no emotional upheaval. Only relief.

First Symptoms*

How Zambodhi experienced it:

This memory is as clear as if the event happened yesterday. Ute seemed to be doing me a favour by allowing me to come with her to this appointment. Like her, I knew the diagnosis was inevitable. We had talked about it several times since her May appointment. Ute thought it made no difference whether I came along or not. She said she couldn't imagine what there was to "support". It certainly felt that way for me when we got there…

After the doctor shared his diagnosis, followed by a quiet "I'm sorry," Ute was sent to a different part of the hospital for another blood sample to be taken. When we got there, a nurse greeted Ute and asked how she was. Ute replied quietly: "I have just received my death sentence." The nurse just continued to speak without paying any attention to Ute's answer. I witnessed it, incredulously and helplessly. It also made me realise that Ute was in shock, of course, although she had expected the diagnosis. The same was true for me. It was unfathomable that Ute had this disease and that it would take her life.

What could I have done? Draw the nurse's attention to Ute's reply? Now, looking back, I wonder how it is possible that patients, after receiving a terminal diagnosis, can just be sent away without even being offered an immediate conversation, or a follow-up discussion where their questions can be answered.

Breaking the News*
[29th August 2014]

Having received the diagnosis, I felt I had to tell everybody. From that moment the times were over when I could deliver a self made explanation for my condition. I used to say: 'I am alright, I just have a serious condition, which has not been diagnosed yet.' With that explanation of my frequent falls in public, there were not too many questions.

The first person I told about my diagnosis was Sam, our farmer[17]. After coming home from the appointment with the consultant, I went down to the farm to do some work in the polytunnel[18] to digest the news. There I met Sam, who was on the tractor just returning some machinery. I told him that I hit the worst-case scenario with confirmed MND. He rightly replied that he didn't know what to say. I found myself saying that I would not give up.

---

17   Sam became a part of the team after Ute had come to the farm. He took on the responsibility for the animals.
18   A polytunnel (also known as a polyhouse, hoop greenhouse or hoop house, grow tunnel or high tunnel) is a tunnel typically made from steel and covered in polyethylene.

I felt the need to tell the farm team first because they would be affected by my increasing disability soon and they already knew best how it stood with me because of working alongside me on the farm. They had first hand observations of all the subtle changes. Up to this point those changes included considerable stiffness, lack of balance on uneven ground, frequent falls caused by the dropping right foot and a loss of physical strength.

Sam was devastated by my diagnosis and I felt I needed to support him in digesting the news. Mark, whom I told the next day, had probably anticipated some bad news. We had previously talked about the changes in my condition during work. At the next shift I shared the news with my line manager and the general manager [at her other workplace, Horsfall House][19].

Prior to that, I had already told them that I was investigating a serious health problem. The general manager suggested to involve the Occupational therapist straight away to adjust the work environment to my deteriorating condition as and when needed. She supported me in my wish to carry on with work for as long as I wished to. Her support never ceased in the years that followed [2011–2014], regardless of my condition. When I could no longer work as a staff nurse, she created a desk-based job as a nurse administrator for me. When I got care dependent, she enabled me to work from home. Only when I could no longer use my fingers on the

---

19 At another place I am sharing my memory of this situation, which is different from Ute's. Ute wanted a fuller picture and in this sense her memory and mine can co-exist with full respect of each other's truth.

Breaking the News*

keyboard, did I finally stop working for Horsfall House – that happened this year in April 2014.

I found it difficult to break the news of my diagnosis to everybody because I also felt obliged to support them so they would not be overwhelmed by it. Their reactions included everything from disbelief to shock and speechlessness to sadness to compassion. That required various strategies of handling. The disbeliever wanted me to get a second opinion and some people really insisted with that. I got emails with contact details of specialists and experts. At the next occasion they checked whether I had acted on their advice. I had no inclination to get a second opinion because I knew my diagnosis was correct. I wanted to get on with my life and did not want to waste my energy and attention on [trying to change] a reality that I couldn't change. Regardless, I had to deal with loads of recommendations. That included dietary advice, contact details for healers and doctors in various countries and lots of links that could be found online. The only information really helpful to me was a copy of a German neurological publication that my mother had received from one of her friends who is a retired neurologist. It was short, concise, fully comprehensive and contained all information I needed.

To the people in shock, I wanted to make clear that I would still be the same person they knew before and that I intended to continue enjoying my life. Sometimes I had to give it all my conviction and positive attitude to reassure them that mine would still be a life worth living, even with MND. The easiest people to talk to were the speechless people because they were closest to my own reality: there was nothing to say, it was better to just get on with life. I didn't like the people, who were convinced that I would just suffer and that I was a poor soul who needed compassion. It did not make sense to me to dwell on my unlucky fate and assume that from now on all I would do would be overshadowed by suffering.

It was difficult for me to repeat the same story – my story – over and over again. For me there was a point at which it became unhealthy to talk about my condition because it enticed me (and others) to define myself exclusively through MND. But I am Ute, and not the disease. Talking over and over again about the same facts created an all dominating reality of terminal illness. But I experienced myself and still do to this present day as a perfectly healthy person living with a serious health condition.

Luckily my sister helped me spread the news, particularly amongst our family. I would have struggled to tell my mother. Towards Christmas, I created a letter in German to be sent to all my friends and relatives on the continent. Five months after having received the official diagnosis, I felt capable of writing about my condition and how it impacted my life from a more neutral perspective. By now I had some experience of living with the disease, which was generally positive. It was important to me that people would get the idea that living with MND was now a normal component of my life and not a life changing catastrophe. MND did change my life but not immediately, rather slowly, little by little. Today, three years after being diagnosed, I am 24/7 care dependent and can not even work on the computer without a carer setting it up for me. Yet, I still feel my normal self. Every day I have things to do or things to look forward to – only the outer conditions have completely changed. My attitude and perceptions remain the same.

Christmas letter to family and friends
Stroud, 10th December 2011

Dear friends,

This year it will be a different letter than the years before. My life is in the process of being completely turned inside out. I live with Motor Neuron Disease.[20] (MND) or in German: Amyotrophic Lateral Sclerosis, ALS for short. Therefore, I will report on living with an illness that inevitably leads to progressive disability and death. However, I must emphasise that I feel perfectly healthy myself, but I am living with a condition that will bring about the complete paralysis of my body.

I'm still amazed at how my strength keeps fading away, a little more every week. Suddenly my leg begins to buckle inward and give out at the knee as if it were made of rubber. There seems to be no cause for this, no injury, no pain, none of the problems that used to be the cause of physical

---

20   Motor neuron diseases (MNDs) are a group of progressive neurological disorders that destroy motor neurons, the cells that control skeletal muscle activity such as walking, breathing, speaking, and swallowing.

impairment in my life up to now. MND is a silent disease. The only outward sign is the constant fasciculations, the constant flickering and twitching of muscles, and that doesn't hurt. But it creates an irritation of body perception, which I would like to call an 'internal noise'. The permanent over-stimulation of the motor nerves leads eventually to their destruction and, as a result, to progressive muscle atrophy. Behind this are hidden inflammatory processes that do not lead to the usual symptoms of inflammation, but which I can see in my eyes and which I observed a year before I had the first physical symptoms, but could not understand at the time. I have cramps from overusing weakened muscles during normal activity. But I can deal with it quite well and don't need any antispasmodic medication.

I'm now at the end of a year, the main hallmark of which is the ongoing dwindling of my strength. Around this time last year I went through a phase of nightly anxiety and restlessness because already then I couldn't attribute the 'noise' in my body to any other disease than MND. I received the official diagnosis in July, and by then I had already gone through my first inner encounters with fear, and the roller coaster ride of hope (it's just my back) and denial (not wanting to believe it - everything is completely different with me). The diagnosis brought clarity and relief. Now it's official, what I am up against, now it is time to live with the disease and find meaning in it all.

At the moment I'm enjoying my active life every day in a new and very conscious way. There are many things I can no

Christmas letter to family and friends Stroud, 10th December 2011

longer do, but there are still more things I can do and that is what I'm concentrating on. I have already said various goodbyes – to the joy of swimming in the sea, hiking the coastal path, climbing up mountains... And fundamentally, walking: I used to move from A to B without knowing what my body was doing, now it is a consciousness exercise. When I walk, my consciousness is in my legs, otherwise I lose my balance, stumble, or fall. And every step is exhausting and costs me a lot of strength.

My intention, my will to do things, is still as quick as ever, but it's crashing into the wall of diminishing physical strength. It's like a physical impact, then I feel nauseous. I have to do an inner check, slow down, and carry on so much slower.

I dread the point of having to give up my physical activities. It's so hard to say when that will be because the body has so many reserves. The disease is progressing steadily, and that day will someday come. How I deal with it and what I do then is beyond my imagination. At the moment I can only face it with trust.

My experience in the nursing profession has shown that it's hardest when things are deteriorating. Once the state of total care dependency is reached, most people have quality of life again, and very few want to die. There is also a universe remaining in the head and that will probably become more active once all external activity ceases. Now I need to take a close look at this, closer than I would have liked with my current consciousness.

Here a difficulty arises. I know the prognosis of MND; I've cared for people with Motor Neuron Disease and I've seen how it can end. If I hold the fact in my mind that I am terminally ill, I can't look forward to trimming the hedge I helped plant last week in a few years, because I know I won't live to see that happen. Or, alternatively, do I live as if my life were endless and accept the tasks that I enjoy, for example in the apprenticeship training? I trust that I will have the time I need to fulfil the tasks that are mine to complete, and that's all I need to hold in my awareness. I am moving between these two perspectives at the moment, whereby I clearly feel how the first one limits my potential, while the second one helps to open up new paths.

I don't take any medication because the effects of Rilutek are uncertain and the medicine is actually still in the trial and error stage. And I don't need medication to control the symptoms because I can live well with my symptoms. I have regular cranial osteopathic therapy which is highly effective when it comes to living with the symptoms. It keeps me emotionally stable, helps me maintain my optimism and gives my body more stability. I probably wouldn't be able to walk any more without the treatment.

At the moment I am still working full time in my two jobs, but I can no longer do certain jobs, especially in agriculture. However, I am in the process of taking on tasks in the apprenticeship program and will probably start working on the farm with young people who do not fit into the school system from next year. Then I will be giving up a shift at Horsfall House.

I pursue all of my hobbies in regular study groups such as the Star group, the Nature Observation Group, the Meditation Group, and the Towards Imagination Group. All groups are about developing and training the perception of the physical and metaphysical world from very different points of view.

All in all, I still enjoy life. But I no longer live as carefree as I did in previous years, because while I have been, as it were, given my death sentence, I do not know when and how it will be carried out. However, one thing is for sure: I will not be deterred from my goals that I want to achieve in life. I want to unfold my skills and potential because I know it matters to others and to myself. And I want to be a happy person. I know the bar is high. Next year will definitely be exciting.

Living and working with MND

[Excerpts from a letter written in October 2012 to the Stroud Agricultural Community, thanking everyone for the donation of money to buy a 'farm proof' mobility scooter for her.]

...Following my diagnosis of MND in July 2011, I continued to work as before, but felt physically tired in the evenings and could no longer do extra hours. I was no longer able to compensate for the deterioration that occurred this year [2011]. Thanks to the way the farm team worked around me – they did all the lifting and other heavy physical work – I was able to keep working. They organised the work to be done so that there was always something I could do.

In June I gave up driving. This meant I needed transport to get to Brookthorpe, [the main part of the farm, a few miles away from Hawkwood College where we lived]. In September I realised I needed a mobility scooter as my left leg had also started to weaken. Without my knowledge, Farmer Sam had already taken the initiative and raised money to procure such a vehicle. The response from farm members and the wider community was overwhelming. The 'Buggy' came in October, just when I really needed it. Since then it has been supplemented with a trailer and a spray device[21]. My ability to walk is now reduced to less than 100 metres, and that is with using walking sticks. With the buggy and the support of the farm team, I can continue working a little longer.

In this situation I experience an impressive aspect of community-supported agriculture, namely the support from the community belonging to the farm. It's not just about celebrating seasonal festivals together and sharing the company's financial risk; it is just as much the sharing of individual situations within the community, no matter whom it affects. This element is very much alive in this community and it helps me to move on and experience joy and fulfilment. And it also helps me focus on what I can still do instead of what I can no longer do.

This is exactly the opposite of what I experienced from health care professionals after I received my diagnosis. They were sorry that I had an illness that would shorten my life expectancy considerably and wanted to comfort me for my losses. They informed me about palliative care, the hospice, and how they could support me in my struggle. The focus was on my deteriorating health, which would inevitably end in my death. But I am fully alive, and I am living a full life, even knowing it will be a little shorter than expected. With this approach I feel supported by you, the community I am part of. A big thank-you to everyone who contributed. I

---

21 A small attachment on two wheels, pulled by the buggy so Ute could operate the spraying device.

don't even know who you all are because it was a surprise gift! I fully believe that this should be celebrated...

The Competition of the Hedgehog and the Hare*
[24th October 2014]

After being diagnosed something began that is comparable with the fairy tale about the competition of the hedgehog and the hare [a Grimm's fairy tale which we enjoyed as children]. The hare with long legs runs and runs but as soon as he approaches the goal the hedgehog comes along and proclaims: I am already here.

Something similar happened with me in trying to compensate for my progressing disability. I got equipment to help me with the foot drop. As a result, I could walk again in an almost normal way. However, soon after I regained normal mobility, I discovered a loss of physical strength. So I saw the osteopath, who helped me to cope with my dwindling strength by [showing me how to lift] my leg high [to avoid catching] my foot—but then, the muscles of my thigh got weaker and I had trouble lifting my leg to hip level.

Thus the typical pattern of MND arose: constant progressive skill loss. I kept adapting through altered techniques and equipment resulting in improved life quality, but that was always followed by further deterioration, which was, in turn, followed by the need to further adapt to the next level of impairment, and so on. This is going on to the present day. Shortly after I find a modus vivendi, the next challenge arises.

The consultant referred me in May 2011 to the orthotist and the MND specialist nurse. The waiting list for an orthotic appointment was six weeks. So I went in June to Cornwall for a holiday without supportive equipment. I bought new shoes which covered my ankle to prevent it from twisting. At that time I did not know that there are [sports] shoes available with supination[22] support, which helps to correct the posture of the knees and the lifting of the foot.

[Instead,] the shoes I had bought [only] helped with the twisting, but the foot drop remained. My sister and brother observed me pulling my right knee high up to get the hanging foot lifted off the ground with every step I did.

> *Stefan, Ute and I went away to Cornwall for our last outdoor holiday together. Ute used to love being outside and doing long hikes through any territory equipped with ordnance survey maps, but that already was no longer an option. We were hoping that she could still walk on footpaths, which she could just about do.*

I walked out of my right hip, which took more energy than typical walking. No surprise that I felt exhausted after

---

22 Supination means that when you walk, your weight tends to be more on the outside of your foot

The Competition of the Hedgehog and the Hare*

only a few hours walking. Silently I said goodbye to walking the coastal path. I knew by next holiday, I would not be able to walk it any more. We stayed at a farm at 'The Lizard', an area of outstanding beauty. We walked a lot but I was always worried whether I would be able to make it back. I had to cope with frequent falls on all occasions.

On our way back home we visited the Lost Gardens of Heligan near St. Austell. There I fell in public without even stumbling and on an even path. People rushed to help me. I was asked the standard question: "are you all right?" I replied with my standard answer: "I am all right but I have a serious condition which has not been diagnosed yet." The witnesses of my fall looked frightened, presumably because it happened so fast and out of the blue.

At that time I was already used to my frequent falls, it was part of my normal life. I had learned to fall without even getting bruised or hurt. At the onset of the disease, falls left me bruised or with lacerations of my skin. It happened so quickly that I could not protect myself. Later my body adapted and the bruising stopped. This way I discovered the remarkable capacity of the human body to adapt. I observed myself falling, it happened still at the same speed but the body reacted on automatic pilot and relaxed completely. It took me a while before I became aware of my body's response. It needed conscious observation to discover that relaxation was the solution to cope with frequent falls. A relaxed body does not get hurt. The year following the diagnosis I fell in all directions and on all grounds but did not get hurt.

This encouraged me to do my personal risk assessment regarding falls: The frequency of falls is high but the impact is low, which puts me overall at low risk. Therefore I decided to carry on with what I was doing and accept the falls as part of my life.

I got a splint fitted to the right foot in August 2011, just before Zambodhi and I went for ten days to Lanzarote. It holds the foot in a right angle to the leg and through its elasticity it boosts the lifting of the foot. I wear these splints on both legs to the present day, now not to ease walking but to keep the feet at the right angle to avoid contracted and stiffened feet in an overstretched position.

Walking with the splint fitted was an amazing experience because I could walk like I used to walk before I got ill. Zambodhi had invited my daughter [Franziska] to Lanzarote to meet us there, which I did not know. What a wonderful surprise when she arrived and what a pleasure to explore the countryside with her and Zambodhi without having to worry about my walking and with far fewer falls. Only swimming in the sea did I have to stay clear of.

The first splint I got I could fit in all my shoes except my wellies. Back home I enjoyed my new freedom of movement at the farm. I saw the physiotherapist in Stroud hospital for an assessment of my mobility. He gave me exercises to strengthen the muscles in my right hip and thigh. The reasoning behind them was to compensate for the muscular waste in that area affected by the disease by developing muscles which were still healthy. I did the exercises for four

The Competition of the Hedgehog and the Hare*

weeks, but they did not help—instead, they only increased the fasciculations in the affected area. I saw the physiotherapist again, and discussed the increasing weakness of my right thigh and the stretch spasm in my right foot in the early morning. We both agreed that forcing exercises would not contribute to my health if it caused fasciculations. We discussed the impact of future deterioration on my motoric capacity. I got a print out for exercises to support breathing and coughing.

Seen with hindsight, none of us had an idea what to expect with further progress of the disease. Today, in October 2014, I struggle with coughing, and the in-breaths I am taking are shorter than they used to be. But how can I do the recommended exercises with a paralysed body? Today I need my carers to help me to clear my throat with clapping [upwards striking movement with the root of the hand on the upper back]. The physiotherapist has to come to my house to teach them what to do.

Next, I got a joint appointment with a physiotherapist and orthotist[23] in anticipation of future muscular waste. The physiotherapist discussed with the orthotist what was expected to happen and what level of support it would require. Because of an old injury, I live without the inner cruciate ligament of my right knee. It was replaced years ago but the replacement only lasted a few years. Because I could compensate for the missing ligament with the well developed

---

23 A healthcare professional who makes and fits braces and splints (orthoses) for people who need to add support for body parts that have been weakened by injury, disease, or disorders of the nerves, muscles, or bones.

muscles of my leg, I left it as it was. Now with MND affecting my leg, my knee was no longer held in its natural position. As a result, my knee was bending inwards. The other knee showed the same tendency; together, they produced an x-shaped gait and both legs rubbed each other. All my trousers got damaged at knee level, and [I] had to use more force for walking.[24]

The professionals involved decided I would need not only a splint up to the knee but something that would hold my knee in position as well to avoid it bending inwards. For that, I had a number of appointments. First to get the foot piece moulded in plaster, next to fit the protheses into my shoes, the third appointment to try to walk with it. But they had blocked the knee so I [would have] developed a stiff leg. Again this needed to be changed and a new appointment was set to try it. The whole process took six months and the prosthesis was heavy, bulky and old fashioned. I could not fit it on without help and it proved too heavy for my dwindling forces. I used it only once.

The farm at Hawkwood is placed on a slope. After our holiday, I discovered in September 2011 that I was losing strength in both my hips. It was exhausting to carry anything uphill or to try to keep up with the other team members

---

24   I did not see a physio again until November 2013 when I got care dependent and my carers complained about the physically challenging moving and handling. The MND nurse had referred me to the neurology physio at Gloucester Royal Hospital because she thought they could advise me more specifically. It took weeks before an appointment came through, which I could not attend. I did not try to get another appointment because of the huge effort for me to go to Gloucester.

The Competition of the Hedgehog and the Hare*

when they walked uphill. The wonderful compensation of the foot drop with the splint was counteracted by my loss of strength.

In July 2012, my sister and I went for a trip to the continent to visit friends in Belgium, Luxembourg and Germany. A friend of mine lent me their walking poles. I found using poles helpful. I could keep my balance a bit better and could transfer some of my weight from my legs to my arms. I went to a sports and outdoor shop in Germany to buy a new pair of shoes and walking poles. The person serving me observed my gait and supplied me with jogging shoes. I was reluctant to try them on because they were not at all my style. But he told me they would support the correct position of both my knees because of built-in supination support. They were designed to use less force to lift the foot off the ground. I tried them on and felt instant relief. My knees and legs did not rub or touch each other, the shoes were extremely light weight, and indeed while walking with them I felt upright again and walking was no longer exhausting. The next few days I felt able to manage five to six kilometres on even ground.

At my next orthotic appointment I asked to get a splint fitted to the other leg, I showed him my shoes and told him how much they changed my gait and how much they reduced my effort to walk. He was not really interested but admitted eventually that they are a nice piece of equipment. Needless to tell him I would have benefited if I would have known before.

In October 2012, I saw the neurologist. I told of my experience with orthotics and that I found shoes by chance which helped me to cope better with my condition. He was not interested either. I find that rather shocking because I know from my time as district nurse how helpful patients' experiences can be. I kept a log of what patients told me to enable myself to recommend it to others whenever appropriate. Why these health professionals showed so little interest I do not understand to the present day. It is far more fun to know all conventional and unconventional ways to cope with a condition such as MND. People are so different, what one person finds helpful does not work for the next.

The most annoying aspect for me was that if I would have known about these shoes when my struggles with walking began, I would have had at least one more year with almost normal walking. But none of the professionals involved in my case gave me a hint about these shoes. I would have loved seeing them paying attention to my experience so that other people could benefit.

By the way: I later supplied my mother with exactly the same shoes because she had a number of serious falls which made her lose her confidence in walking. I had observed her inwardly rotated knees, resulting in a shuffling gait. After putting on those shoes, both symptoms disappeared instantly. I have not heard of further falls ever since.

After I saw the neurologist in October 2012, things went quiet. I did not see the MND nurse who used to visit every four to six weeks. In March 2013 I tried to get in touch with

The Competition of the Hedgehog and the Hare*

her and found out that was leaving at the end of the month. Her post was expected to be vacant for six months. (The new MND nurse introduced herself in January 2014.)

On her first visit the original MND nurse referred me to the neurology OT[25] from Gloucester Royal Hospital for a home visit to discuss supportive equipment. That was in Autumn 2011. After a few weeks an appointment came through and I have seen the neurology OT from Gloucester Royal Hospital once or twice. She supplied me with a slide sheet, which stays in bed on top of the mattress. This helped me to slide my increasingly stiffening right leg from one side to the other. I kept socks on at night to support the sliding process. With this I was able to turn my legs out of the movement of my hip. She supplied a trolley to enable me to walk without the splint in our flat. The trolley had two shelves, which I used to transport what I would have otherwise held in my hands. I was not overly happy with her support because I only got what I requested.

> *How would Ute have got these aids, had she not known about them already and therefore been able to ask for them? Why was she not offered them without having to ask?*

In early 2012 I rang Stroud Social Services Adult Helpdesk and enquired what to do in case of further deterioration and increased disability. The perspectives were not encouraging

---

25   Occupational therapist (OT) responsible for assessment and intervention to develop, recover, or maintain the meaningful activities, or occupations, of individuals, groups, or communities.

and not at all clear, predominantly because nobody could anticipate how my skill losses would develop. But they send me the OT [working in the local community] for an initial assessment. This was the beginning of a very supportive and effective relationship. Whenever I had a problem I could call her. She rang me back within a day when she was out of office. She got equipment in, bit by bit, as my physical capacity diminished. When the left leg started to get paralysed, she got my bed raised and had a grab-rail fitted to the bed. With the help of the grab rail I could transfer some of my action from the legs to my arms which still had full strength. I got a bath board to enable me to get out of the bath, and a perching chair for the kitchen to give a stable base for domestic work. Later I got a toilet frame. All this equipment came my way as I discussed my present problems and she responded.

The most pressing question soon became, "where was I going to live when I am no longer able to make the stairs?" This question remained unresolved. I did not want to leave the College because it was home to one half of our farm, on which I continued to work. Plus, there were always people around whom I could call when I needed help. In the other flat [on site at the College] was a big downstairs room, which could be suitable for my needs but I did not know whether it would become available. In the meantime the OT got handrails fitted to our staircase. Now I dragged my legs up the stairs with my arms. I was leaning my body onto the wall, grabbing one leg with both hands and lifting it onto the next step. Then I put my hands on the hand rails to both sides of

The Competition of the Hedgehog and the Hare*

the staircase and pulled myself up onto the next step. Next I pulled the other leg up.

I asked for a wheelchair because I knew I would need one when I could no longer use my legs. With my diagnosis I qualified for a powered wheelchair, which needs a proper assessment by the wheelchair service. This service is very busy, the waiting list is about six weeks. I was assessed in April 2013. In Gloucestershire the MND Society provides two powered wheelchairs with a high level of support to ensure people with MND get it close to their point of need and do not have to wait until after initial assessment for a wheelchair is funded, ordered and delivered. One of those wheelchairs has proven to be right for me, but because I lived upstairs they took it back with them. (I was assessed as still being able to walk upstairs, and therefore they determined I did not really need a wheelchair.)

I was worried about what would happen when I could no longer walk. The wheelchair service did not have an answer to that question. They could only provide what I was entitled to according to my assessment. If I had been living in a ground floor flat, things may have been different. Again I discussed this with my OT and, thanks to her, got a self propelled wheelchair the same week.

In Autumn 2013, I asked for the powered wheelchair again. It took another six weeks until delivery although it was marked as urgent. My situation got more and more precarious. I could only walk short distances on crutches. At the farm I used the buggy. For getting to work at the nursing home I used a taxi and around the house the manual wheelchair.

> *Climbing up the stairs to the flat I now needed help lifting my legs to the next step because I needed to keep holding on to the rails as my whole body was so unstable.*[26]

In this situation the family of our farmer, who had just moved into a bungalow in Brookthorpe [the other site of the farm] offered me to stay with them until I found a home. Again the OT went with me to assess the bungalow and ordered the necessary alterations and equipment. A temporary ramp was installed, a profiling bed and toilet frame ordered. The day after my sister had to first drag me up the stairs, I moved to Brookthorpe. This was in July 2013. But I did not know where to move to [next], and I was anyway not able to look for accommodations. Difficult decisions had to be made.

For seven years I had shared a one bedroom flat with my sister. Now I felt I had to find something [either] for myself or with her within a larger community. The decision making process was quite painful. [After we made the decision that we would no longer live together] My sister was offered accommodation at her work place, while I had no idea how to solve my problem with accommodation. I registered with

---

26 Videolink to the latter stage of this process, when someone else was needed to lift Ute's legs as her arms had become too weak. This video was taken just before the process became impossible and she had to move out. https://youtu.be/a7ZPeStTayY

The Competition of the Hedgehog and the Hare*

Gloucestershire home seekers, the social housing scheme in Gloucestershire. I was prioritised to the gold band which is only one step below emergency. But in the three months I was included in the social housing scheme, I got no concrete offer.

Stroud district council was more alert. They offered a flat in sheltered housing in Stonehouse and a bungalow in Chalford. While I was in Brookthorpe the Bungalow next to the one that I was staying in became vacant, but the landlord did not want to rent it out again because of its poor condition. While I was staying with the farmers family my condition worsened rapidly and became precarious. I could no longer care for myself. I needed help. The situation with the family was at the point of breakdown. I had to surrender and call social services to help me urgently. In the morning of September the 27th 2013 I left a message with my allocated social worker and the OT. The OT responded and found within hours a place for me in a reablement unit in Gloucester. In the early afternoon I visited the place with her and after the weekend, two days later, I moved in there. Again the OT took care that the right bed was provided and ordered on request of the home the right shower chair.

> *Ute needed assistance for her personal care at this point. It had become high risk trying to do it on her own. The family of four with only one bathroom and school children could not absorb someone needing the bathroom for longer periods of time several times a day when their busy lives began again after the Summer holidays.*

While I was staying there my sister and friends joined their efforts to find a home for me. Luckily someone managed to convince the landlord to let me rent the bungalow in Brookthorpe. At the same time a bungalow in Chalford became available. The OT had seen it and decided it was suitable. Together we went to see the Bungalow in Brookthorpe, which was indeed in a poor state of repair. The wooden floors were broken, the walls and ceilings showed big cracks, the carpet was worn out, and altogether it was in need of decoration. Compared to Chalford, this was not appropriate. But it was close to the farm in the middle of beautiful nature in the Severn valley, close to the outskirts of the Cotswolds hills. My friends promised to bring the house up to an acceptable status within a fortnight, which they indeed achieved. The OT could see that this bungalow could meet my needs, so she negotiated with the landlord necessary alterations such as a ramp to the front door, widening of the toilet door, and a wheelchair suitable path. This is a miracle in my view: an OT who prioritises my social needs and who trusts my friends to renovate the house in time. And indeed on November the 4[th,] 2013 I moved in with a massive care package.

At first the Stroud Enablement Team came with two carers four times a day to assist me with personal care and toileting at home. At night I had a carer from a different agency, to assist me at night with positioning. Some of the Reablement workers struggled with the handling of my increasingly paralysed body and often called OT and physiotherapist in to assess the situation. The physiotherapist introduced exercises

The Competition of the Hedgehog and the Hare*

[for carers to perform on] my paralysed legs and stretch exercises for my feet to avoid a shortening of the Achilles tendon. The exercises made a difference within a week. Both feet were less stiff. I became aware that my limbs need to be moved passively because they no longer had any active movement.

For my left foot this insight and the intervention of the Physio came a bit late; the ankle got already partly permanently stiff. This is called a contracture. Unfortunately, this often happens with immobilised parts of the body. In my case it happened during the process of paralysation. I had frequent stretch spasms during that time. Often I could not bring the foot back in its normal flexed position because the other leg was already paralysed. With the right leg, which got paralysed first, I could avoid the stiffening of the ankle by jumping out of bed and transferring my full body weight on that foot when the stretch spasm happened. I also did stretching exercises in a standing position to keep the Achilles tendon at full function.

Since I have carers coming into my home the physiotherapist visits from time to time to give carers exercises for my paralysed limbs, the partly stiff ankle is the only permanent damage I have at the time of this writing. My hands and wrists are soft and relaxed but hypotone[27]. I have experimented with splints [to prevent contractures of hands and wrists].

I requested night splints for my feet as soon as I became aware of the stiffening of my ankle. That needed online

---

27   Hypotone – medical term for reduced muscle tone

research and negotiations with the orthotist. It did not help; I could not wear them at night because it was too painful and I could not turn onto my side with splints on. I also tried to get a splint moulded by a specialised OT in Stroud hospital. This splint I could use for a number of hours before it became painful. As it was not strong enough to withstand stretch spasms, it disintegrated after a while, producing sharp edges which damaged the bedding.

The metal day splints [preventing the Achilles tendons from shortening] I wear to the present day without any problems.

Hand and finger splints: My left hand started to paralyse at the turning of 2013/14. Again this was accompanied by flex spasms of the hand. I needed to open my fingers with my other hand but they went back into a curled position as soon as I removed my hand. The splinting expert from Stroud hospital came out upon my request and moulded a splint for my left hand. Again I could not wear it at night because I did not know how to position the arm at night, and the splint lost its straps within days.

Because my speech deteriorated I have used a typewriter since February 2014. This little machine consists of a keyboard that allows me to type what I wanted to say and transforms it into spoken words. I got quickly used to it and had extended conversations using the typewriter.

As happened over and over with this disease I had a few weeks of freedom with this method before it stopped working for me. I was able to express myself verbally with the

The Competition of the Hedgehog and the Hare*

typewriter as I liked, but soon, due to progressing paralysis of arms, hands and fingers this became at first increasingly difficult and eventually impossible. To slow this deterioration I got finger splints for selected fingers of both hands to enable me to continue typing both on the computer and typewriter. That gave me another month, but it was hard work. I had to give up the computer at the beginning of April.

Up until then I worked two days per week from home for the local nursing home, but that was the end of me doing employed work.

However, thankfully, I was well supported by my speech and language therapist. She came out and supplied me with a mouse-controlled writing program for the computer. After two weeks I was back on the computer, using a mouse-controlled software and a virtual, onscreen keyboard.

My hands are fully paralysed today (October 2014) and so are my arms. I can pull my left arm a bit with the remaining function of my biceps, but that is all. My splint expert from Stroud hospital has supplied me with off the shelf [hand] splints, which I wear during the day. The physiotherapist has come out to show my carers stretch exercises for my hands. My hands are fully relaxed because I use the splints. Without splints they curl up into a fist within half an hour. At night the carer stretches my hands onto my thighs where they remain unchanged provided I don't cough.

The next part of my body the physio has to look at is my head.

> *Ute was losing the use of her neck muscles, leaving her head with a tilt which caused discomfort. Again, the race against time began; to acquire as soon as possible a bespoke headrest that had to be made to hold her head reasonably upright but resting in a corner of the headrest. See photo in Foreword.*

Work*
[11th August 2014]

At the time of diagnosis, the most noticeable health changes had already become apparent at the farm. In 2009, I was once unloading crates with vegetables from an open trailer that had rotten flooring in some places. I broke through the flooring and hurt my foot. I remember this clearly because we discussed amongst the farm team my lack of spatial awareness but not the rotten flooring. In spring 2010, I went with Sam and a backpack sprayer [with shoulder straps] to apply biodynamic preparations on the land. I can not remember what I did but as a result I lost balance, and the weight of the sprayer filled with 15 litres of water pulled me down. I landed like a beetle on my back and like a beetle I was unable to get up. Sam, laughing, said he deeply regretted not having a camera at hand before he helped me up. At the time I also was laughing. I had no explanation why that happened but seen with hindsight this is typical with MND.

During 2010, the major issue was the loss of strength. I struggled to operate a rotavator[28]; I also could not load

---

28   Rotavator - is used to dig up the soil, turn it over and then rake it level.

extended loads on a wheelbarrow and push it uphill. Given the fact that I am female, nobody expected me to do the heavy-duty work and took it on without question, but I noticed the changes, because I used to be able to do this without problem.

In July 2010, I went to an osteopath for treatment of my right foot and to help with the frequent falls I had by then. The treatment helped with the actual problem but due to the progressing disease there was soon another problem needing to be dealt with. Some of my regular jobs got increasingly difficult. For example stringing up tomatoes and cucumbers in the polytunnel became a challenge for my weakening balance. I had to climb a bench like children do: first on my knees and then using the support of my hands to get up in order to be able to hook the strings up onto the overhead wire. The year before, I simply overstretched a bit and hooked them on with a little jump, or I used a broken milk crate to climb on.

2011 was the first year of me consciously saying goodbye to a number of skills and work activities. Making hay was one of them. The beloved hay making season had, all my adult life, been the most exciting time of the year. Walking the coastal path was another activity I could no longer do. Then I had to say goodbye to setting up a compost heap by hand, walking in the furrows of the potato field, carrying a rucksack type sprayer on my back – the list is long...

In December 2011, we planted a hedge in a sloping field at the boundary of our land. To prepare for the planting the

Work*

grass had to be mown and the strip had to be rotavated. I volunteered to do the mowing with the big lawn mower. This was already a bit too heavy for me but downhill and with two people watching me it worked. I needed their help to restart the lawnmower because I did not have the strength to pull the starter string. The people watching me were certainly a bit worried, but for me it was consciously saying goodbye to using the lawn mower.

I knew I would never use it again.

On that occasion my weakness had progressed so far that I was unable to walk at the same pace like everyone else on the uphill slope out of the field. This was another new experience having to be left behind because of my slowness. From then on I was grateful for every lift with a car I could get. But climbing into a farm four-wheel-drive vehicle turned out to be another challenge. My colleagues helped as much as they could, when I needed help to climb into a vehicle or had lost my balance. They got used to my frequent falls and seemed to have learned to accept them as part of my present life. Gradually, as we all got used to it, they no longer asked me: "Are you ok?" when I fell, but instead: "Another one of the usual?" before they helped me up again. This helped me to accept the increasing disability as an integral part of my life.

By 2012, I could do less and less and got progressively slower. I liked working with the wheel hoe[29] and the long-handled hand hoe because they gave me more stability;

---

29   Wheel hoe – tool to push through rows (fields or garden) garden to weed, till, cultivate, or plough.

in the spring I could still work with the big-wheel hoe but it exhausted me. During the summer it became hand-hoeing only. Doing hand weeding, I crawled along the rows. I had always done it on my knees, but now I noticed that I needed my hands to support my body, which left only one hand free for weeding while I was moving along the row. I still had full strength in my arms and upper body but I had to separate moving my legs forward from doing the work with my hands. The same applied for harvesting spinach or lettuce.

My colleagues worked more and more around me and prepared my work environment. When it was me who cut the lettuce, someone else had to place the crates in the field and collect the full ones after the work was done. Working in the polytunnel became increasingly challenging. The picking of beans in June was not a problem yet, but the harvesting of tomatoes in September was, because I had to reach up for picking and to bend down for collecting them in the crate while I had nothing to hold on to. When I did the planting of the winter salads, I was in danger of damaging the plants because I dragged my legs behind me while using my arms to move forward.

The next thing that would inevitably happen would be that I could not get up [without help from someone else]. I dreaded it because it would have to be the end of my working with the soil. It became more difficult by the week. I tried to use hoes, crates or posts in the polytunnel to pull myself up with my hands. The first time I needed to ask for help to get up happened in cold, rainy weather in November. Soon after,

Work*

one beautiful day in December 2012 it was over: I could not get up any more in the polytunnel. Now I had to say goodbye to my beloved farm work. At least I had reached my target to continue working until the end of the year.

From now on I worked only Tuesday and Friday afternoon in the packing shed helping to prepare the share. To enable me to do that the other team members had to collect my perching chair[30] and set me up in the packing shed. Sitting on this raised chair I had both (!) hands free to work. But I could no longer work on my own, I needed a second person who prepared the crates with vegetables within the reach of my hands and who took the readily packed vegetables away. But even when all of that was set up, my joy about still being able to do some meaningful work was undisturbed.

Until my hands began to deteriorate. It started with the arm which got stiff and somehow weak, similar to the stiffness due to cold weather. And indeed cold weather aggravated the problem. But soon it was obvious the disease had reached my hands. A little bit later things fell out of my hands. I could no longer grab four potatoes at once with my hands. I had to bend down frequently to pick up items which I had dropped. My whole working life followed a certain pattern given by the disease: adaptation, work is still enjoyable, further weakening of muscles making work ever harder followed by the need for further adaptation to the next level of skill loss. Because I was not willing to give up anything before

---

30   Perching chair – high chair to perch on supporting body weight and balance.

I absolutely had to, working became tougher for me. But that was still better than not doing the work any more.

July 2013 was the end of my work in the packing shed and the end of my active work on the farm. Now I only continue to tutor the apprentice.

Voice and Feelings*
[24th August 2014]

One of the most intimate instruments to express our personality is the human voice. In our voice lives a piece of our soul, which allows other people to have a direct perception of our emotional state. We are used to perceiving this message of soul automatically alongside spoken words. Most people are not even aware of this happening. In our culture we perceive information about distress, joy, danger, sadness, importance and other issues through the tone of the voice more than through the actual words spoken. We can express tenderness, love and calmness with our voice, and we can use this capacity to help a child or a person in distress to calm down. Similarly, with the pitch of our voice we can upset others. And also, we can use our voice to sing. Again with our singing voice we convey a full range of feelings – the calming effect of a lullaby, the aggressive tone of songs in some football matches, the self-empowering songs of soldiers, the devotion of a church choir, the cheerfulness of a birthday song at the party and many others. One of the mysteries of our voice is the fact that we perceive our own voice from within, while we hear all other voices with our ears from without. Most people are surprised how different their voice sounds when they hear it recorded.

I used to sing in a church choir when I lived in Belgium. During those years my singing voice unfolded a certain fullness; I loved to give my voice something to do. In unobserved moments particularly in spaces with good acoustic, I sang whole heartedly giving my voice full freedom. I was not a good singer because I had difficulties with counting, but my hearing is good. I had no problem finding and keeping the right pitch. That was important to me.

In 2012, my speech finally began being affected by the disease. Speech is composed of voice and articulation. We articulate in our mouth using tongue, teeth and lips. In early Spring 2012, I noticed a weakness in the middle of my upper lips. This was accompanied by a kind of delay in articulation of some consonants. It was again the same pattern as with all the other skill losses: suddenly articulation did not happen as an unobserved automatic function of my mouth organs any more. I had to consciously initiate articulation of certain consonants. First nobody apart from myself noticed. After two months my sister noticed. By that time I sometimes had to slow down and repeat a word because it didn't come out correctly. I noticed the weak spot became broader and the middle of my lower lip started to be affected. It felt as if my lips got limp. Outwardly nothing was visible yet but I had the feeling of broken lips. My sister started to video some of my talks to preserve a memory of me talking. In the Summer

Voice and Feelings*

2012 people started to ask me occasionally to repeat a word, which I needed to get used to. Slowly I discovered that not only my lips but also my tongue was changing. I could not move my tongue to the sides of my mouth as I used to.

2013 brought major impairments. The year before I could compensate by articulating consciously and sometimes repeating a word. Now I experienced major losses. My speech became blurred at times and people asked me frequently to repeat words. During our holidays in July we visited a little church in Belgium. As usual we sang a round to honour the place and enjoy the acoustic. To my surprise my voice dropped on its own. I tried to get back to the right pitch but I couldn't. I was utterly shocked. I realised the disease has now captured my voice. No more singing because dropping in pitch sounds horrible.

From this event onwards it went downhill very fast. I was still living with the family of our farmer. In his household everyone sang. Sometimes the blessing of the meals was sung. Singing before the meal one day in September not only dropped my singing voice in pitch but it broke completely. I was deeply disturbed and ended up in tears. Losing my ability to walk and being wheelchair dependent was nothing compared to losing my voice. Walking can be replaced with a wheelchair but how could I replace my voice? I had the feeling I had to let go of a skill which is an integral part of myself. In my voice there is my soul.

At the same time the pitch of my speaking voice dropped as well. To me it felt as though it was no longer my own voice.

Hearing myself speaking it really felt like 'that is not me'. Articulation also became even more difficult. Certain words, such as museum, I could no longer pronounce at all. With my broken lip seal[31] it was impossible to form the sound M. Suddenly the number of words I could use shrank. I needed to think about how I could express what I wanted to with a dwindling vocabulary.

In October 2013, I was confronted with the total loss of my voice. I was overwhelmed by a feeling of sadness following a remark somebody had made about my attitude to disability. I was sobbing but I could not say a word. The people attending me begged me to tell them what had happened. I was under pressure but had no speech. Eventually I got a piece of paper and wrote down that I could not speak. Once I settled a bit I wrote about the event and its impact on me. This was the beginning of expressing myself [my daily needs] by writing.

Since October 2013 I have needed care. Obviously not only my speech was affected but my ability to eat deteriorated alongside it. This disturbed my sense of dignity more than anything else. With carers attending me I had to communicate to people who did not know me. It became more difficult because most of them didn't know how to use slide sheets and how to move a body with limbs that are not firmly connected to their sockets, due to muscular waste. The resulting moving and handling caused increasing distress both for

---

31   Lip seal - the ability to hold the lips together securely, preventing food, drink and saliva from reemerging.

Voice and Feelings*

my carers and me. In distress my speech got more slurred than usual, causing even more distress. Being frightened of painful moving and handling and unable to articulate sufficiently I started to scream. Rightly my carers demanded of me to calm down, which I did not always manage to do because I was too frightened. With this half a year of very difficult communication started.[32]

At Christmas time, people who didn't know me well struggled to understand me. It became more and more a guessing game to figure out what I was saying. I knew what I wanted to say and as an inner process it was of course still well articulated and clear. People picked the words they understood and guessed the rest. Because they did not feed back to me what they thought I wanted to say but just said that they understood, I had no idea whether I got the message across or not.

Usually most people do not want to disappoint the person they are talking to by admitting that they don't understand. I count myself in, because I have often nodded or simply confirmed with one or other 'yes', at times when I did not understand aphasic[33] clients for example. I have tried to catch the one or other word and tried to guess the content of the person's speech according to what I believed I heard the person saying. Now I found people were doing this to me. It is

---

[32] Ute was in temporary care for 4 weeks in October 2013. In November she moved into her bungalow and two care agencies took on to look after her. In the Spring of 2014 Denise became the manager of the daycare agency and then finally things became stable with a selected team working with Ute. That the loss of her voice happened during that time made things even harder for her and others.
[33] Aphasic – when a person has difficulty with their language or speech.

difficult to discern what people understand as long as they get part of the message, but it is easy to recognize when someone does not understand at all. Then the non verbal connection between me and the person listening is disrupted. The whole communication appears to be hollow.

In January 2014, I wrote key words or sentences down, which was difficult because my right hand was so much affected by weakness. I had to kind of draw each letter[34], because writing as I had known it, without even thinking about the movement part of the activity, was no longer possible. In February I got my first speech-typewriter. This improved my communication a great deal. I kept the typewriter on my lap and typed everything I wanted to say. This was faster than handwriting or having to repeat words over and over again. Most beneficial was that it brought clarity back into my communication.

I had two good months before it started to become difficult again. My hands were giving up little by little. I struggled to slide my hands over the keyboard and get my fingers to type. I had to use predictive text wherever possible. That worked well with the English typewriter but not with the German one. German is not suitable for prediction because of the three different sexes which requires different endings for a lot of words.

---

34 See photo in the next chapter.

Voice and Feelings*

> *Ute used mostly using English and eventually exclusively, because it needs fewer and has shorter words available. But she kept reading in German as well as English. When she had visitors from Belgium, Austria and Germany she wrote in German as long as she could use the typewriter. Between us communication had shifted to English already. About three months before she died and after she had been unable to speak at all for some months Ute wrote to me "I love being bilingual" Had she written this in German it would have been "Ich liebe es Zweisprachig zu sein."*

As with all other areas, deterioration carried on: first it became harder to use the typewriter, but still doable. Then I got exhausted from doing it and eventually I could not do it at all without help. Only two of my carers could manage to help me by sliding my finger over the keyboard and pressing down where I indicated with my eyes but most could not read my eye movements. Again, I experienced situations of not being able to communicate. The worst case was, when I was supplied with the typewriter and the supplying person did not even realise that I could not lift my arms to reach the keyboard. This carer proceeded to encourage me to cooperate and I tried to indicate that I needed help to do so and eventually I ended up screaming in despair. This happened also when I could see something going wrong, for example trying to pass a door with extended wheelchair control. Frequent experiences of that kind increased my level of anxiety considerably.

In June 2014, I got my eye-gaze equipment, which allowed me to operate the computer with my eyes. Together with a program which transformed the written word into spoken word, I was able to communicate to my needs again. I could take part in discussions, prepare contributions for meetings beforehand and store them until needed. I could keep my diary, do my emails and all the other activities I usually do with the computer. The only downside was that it kept me stationary, bound to the computer in my living room. The eye gaze camera turned out to be extremely sensitive picking up either other people's eye or body movements or the wind in the trees outside. It doesn't like sunlight, so I disappeared behind drawn curtains which I am not at all fond of. Dull weather and artificial light provided better speaking conditions.

The last factor in the equation is the tiredness of my eyes. I take atropine to dry my hyper salivation, which dilates my pupils, making my eyes more sensitive to light. Focussing for hours on a white screen is draining. All these various factors limit the time I spend in front of the screen, which limits the amount of time I am able to communicate.

Anger and Grief

[probably January 2014]

[From a conversation in German, of which Ute's handwritten part was found, written probably in the turn of 2013/2014, when she had a friend from Austria with her.]

It is easier to panic or be angry than to allow grief. That would overwhelm me. Therefore I would rather be angry. Anger overshadows the deeper feeling. Which is sadness. I'm right in the middle of it.

This is what is meant by following Christ. Not my will but Thy will be done. This has nothing to do with suffering. I am not suffering. I have only been given the greatest difficulties to overcome.

I do not know if this [illness] is for me or for something else. I only know that I wanted to work on the development of the earth and I was given this task. People see the spirit world shining through here. That's why they say, "You look good, you are an inspiration." Then something else happens. I lose my body as an instrument and at the same time become an instrument for something higher. I did ask and was accepted.

Finding Connection and Fulfillment in the Face of Motor Neuron Disease

> Es ist einfacher Panik zu haben oder wütend zu sein als die Trauer zuzulassen. Das würde mich überwältigen. Also bin ich lieber wütend. Die Wut überlagert das eigentliche Gefühl, das ist Trauer. Da bin ich mitten drin.
>
> Das ist gemeint mit Nachfolge Christi. Nicht mein Wille sondern Dein Wille geschehe. Das hat mit Leiden nichts zu tun. Ich leide nicht, ich habe nur grösste Schwierigkeiten zu überwinden.
>
> Diese Weg der Krankheit — ob das nun für mich ist oder für etwas anderes weiss ich nicht. Ich weiß nur daß ich an der Entwicklung dieser Erde mitarbeiten wollte und diese Aufgabe habe ich bekommen.
>
> Die Leute sehen hier die geistige Welt durchschen. Deshalb sagen sie, du siehst gut aus, du bist eine Inspiration. Dann passiert etwas anderes: Ich verliere meinen Körper als Instrument + werde gleichzeitig zu einem Instrument für etwas Höheres.
>
> Ich habe gefragt + bin angenommen worden.

The Challenge of Communication*

[A selection of Ute's reports about the key role of communication through the year 2014, when she experienced the loss of all her physical independence and became completely reliant on assistance.]

Night Experiences*
[10th August 2014, written for the book]

Thanks to my interrupted nights, I was able to watch the morning birds sing nearly every day for four years. To my surprise, they did not start singing when it was still dark, but waited until the first third of dawn had passed and stopped again during the last third of dawn.

In the Summer of 2013 I lost the ability to change my position in bed. I needed care during the night. Since then I have had to ask for help whenever I needed to change my position. Throughout my adulthood I always slept on my side. I couldn't fall asleep lying on my back. For the last ten years I have preferred to fall asleep on my left side. I woke up in the morning lying on this side, and I suppose I didn't turn over during the night. Whether this is normal or was an early sign of the disease I don't know. Looking back, I remember various details that might have been early signs of the illness, such as twitching in my eyelid, tight clenching of my jaw on waking, and spasms in the stomach area.

When I got care at night, the carers turned me from one side to the other into recovery position [as in a first aid positioning]. I managed two hours on my preferred side and one hour on the other one. That quickly changed to lying only on the good side and being turned onto my back and eventually I could lie on my back only. Due to muscular waste my shoulders got so weak that I could no longer tolerate lying on my side. We got the OT and the physiotherapist in to find out if positioning on my sides would work when supported with specially designed positioning cushions but nothing worked well for longer than a few weeks.

At the same time my speech deteriorated. During the day the typewriter worked perfectly well but at night I struggled. When turned onto my side I could not use it; I needed to be sat up in bed in order to be able to use it.

Deteriorating speech and the fact that I was dependent on carers and their varying skill levels brought a new factor into my nights: anxiety. That started with the use of a slide sheet which most carers didn't know how to use correctly. I have been the moving and handling trainer in the nursing home where I have been working. This now turned to be a curse and a blessing at the same time. I could train the carers attending me in the appropriate use of slide sheets, that was the blessing. But I noticed every detail which was not correct, what avoidable discomfort it caused me and even worse I anticipated what would go wrong in the next moment and that was the curse. Because of my increasingly limited communication I started to scream when I could not make myself understood.

Night Experiences*

Ute sometimes howled or quietly wept rather than screamed, when she was devastated about the assumptions people made, instead of assisting her with communication first. I had to teach those carers who did not know Ute well enough, that she always had a reason when she screamed, that it was a warning that something was going wrong and causing her harm. Night care was provided by a different care agency. The night carers did not know Ute well at all because they came in when she was supposed to sleep and assist with her needs during the night. Eventually Ute also got a dedicated night team and both care agencies worked well together. These problems happened when someone was put into her rota who had no experience with this sort of complexity and risk (below an example of it in day time).

Ute's devastation about losing the ability to speak was all-pervading, She wept many times when it overwhelmed her. I remember when our Mother had come for a visit with our brother and we were having a meal. Ute could just about feed herself still but chewing and swallowing were challenging and because she was losing the muscles in her cheeks they became floppy and she accidentally bit them, which was very painful. Her articulation was very difficult to understand at that time. Ute wheeled herself out of the room while we were trying to reassure her that her "messy eating" was no problem for us and that she didn't need to feel ashamed about it. Ute screamed and left the room. Afterwards we found out that she had just bitten her cheek accidentally for the third time and that she was in so much pain that she could no longer bear to eat while food kept falling out of her mouth, nor the frustration about not being understood when she tried to say what had happened.

Terrifying Care Experience

[1st May 2014 direct communication for the care agency]

Two carers came who did not know my morning routine. During washing and dressing me in the bed they didn't bend my leg, but overstretched my knee instead, causing pain in hip and knee. Poor moving and handling on turning me with slide sheets left my legs in the wrong position. They ended up tipping me on my face. They didn't notice that, whilst they washed my back and bottom, I was tilted onto my face, which compromised my breathing.

They hoisted me out of the bed in a lying position and kept me in a lying position on the toilet sling. They tried to put my shoes on while I was in that position in the hoist. I screamed because of back pain. They didn't stop. Then they put my upper body on the bed while I was still in that position in the hoist and put the shoes on. The left foot was not in the shoe properly, the right big toe was rolled up in the shoe, and the right leg was twisted to the right during the whole procedure, causing pain in my right hip. All the straps were too tight. Then they transferred me onto the shower chair. I had no access to communication and they simply carried on. They put the trousers on and then finally I got the light writer back and asked them to loosen the straps, which they did. In the bathroom they were unable to position me onto the shower chair, so that I could help to pull the trousers up and they didn't give me the typewriter to tell them how to position me correctly. They didn't manage to position me at the sink for me to rinse my teeth.

When they transferred me out of the bathroom, they didn't put my feet on the footrest. My feet got dragged over the floor and got stuck under the chair when I was moved forward. Christina [one of the main carers just arriving for her day shift] saw it and saved me.

I had refused to have my shoes put on in bed, because the left foot needed a T A stretch, which is done in sitting position. They didn't give me the chance to explain this and to let them know that this is done with me in the shower chair. I was completely exhausted and Christina had some work to do to put things right.

My Unspoken Needs*
[16th June 2014]
[Selected direct communications with carers on the night team]

Last night I woke up with a stiff neck because the pillow was too much down on my shoulders, which tilted my head too much. I had residual fluids in my throat and no control over my voice and the noises I was making. Attending carers obliged me to settle down. I felt a wave of despair for again being told off for something I am not in control of because it is a symptom of my disease.

I have bulbar symptoms that affect my voice, swallowing and residual fluids. With increasing paralysis, I feel as if I am jammed in a block of concrete. It costs me a lot of strength to endure it. The noise I am making has partly to do with my battle with the concrete, partly with a slight obstruction in my throat due to my tilted head and partly with the disease. I can quieten the sounds for a couple of breaths, but then they are back again and I have to put up with it.

Day staff recognize my noise as an indication of my discomfort and approach me with empathy. Night staff appear to be offended and expect me to calm down. I have to suppress my body expression as best I can to avoid trouble. It makes me cry quietly and I try to resolve my discomfort myself. I am often asked why I don't take painkillers. I do take a painkiller when I am in pain but they don't help against the feeling of being poured in a block of concrete, the inability to clear the throat or being bloated like last night.

When I had my tea this morning, I had the cup between my teeth so I couldn't drink. I tried and obviously bit the cup and was told off. Next time I didn't drink and was told off for not drinking. I avoided any shouting, I didn't request the type writer because I am more or less unable to type. When I try to be quiet, I depend on staff picking up subtle observations. I did not bite the cup because I am naughty but because it is between my teeth [and that triggers a biting reflex].

I have often asked for the cup to be held close to my lower lips and to tilt it high enough so the tea goes down. Today I was asked to hold my head back. I have not enough head control left to do such movements, I need staff to assist me.

Because of my deterioration I cannot do things that I was still able to do last week. Because I am unable to speak, I can do nothing but rely on staff observing my skill loss and making the necessary adaptations. I know this is a challenge for all of us.

The difficulties got resolved by a meeting with the team manager, myself and the district nurse. Particularly one team member, who was brilliant as long as I could talk, found it difficult to pick up on my non-verbal communication. She stopped attending to me at night. With the present regular night carers, I have a good connection. I continue to write to them to update them about my condition, change of routine or cause of strange behaviour last night.

> *[Written communication with carers* **18th June 2014***]*
>
> *Due to progressive paralysis of my hands I am almost unable to use the typewriter. You need to help me and supply me with my [finger] splints. I will only be able to use certain keywords. I use the computer for communication. The eye-gaze equipment is up and running. Care staff need training to set it up for me and I need more practice. For [communication aid at] night I am waiting for low tech-letter charts. I will refurbish the communication charts. Any phrases you want on there please let me know.*

Desperation in communication or the Lion in the Cage*
[19th June 2014]
[follow up information for care agency]

I cannot use the typewriter anymore, my hands are too paralysed now. That means I am without verbal communication, unless I sit at the computer. In all day-to-day care situations I am mute. This creates the feeling of a lion caught in a cage. I try to communicate non verbally via pointing with my head and eyes but most of the time nobody notices. Then I scream to draw people's attention. Carers are stressed when I scream because they don't know what is wrong but they always think I am in pain. Because they didn't notice my subtle attempts to communicate non verbally, they think I scream straight away and want me to calm down. This hurts me so much because I try my utmost to draw attention to what I need assistance with non verbally.

Today while on the toilet I accidentally hit the call bell while I was coughing. I shook my head to indicate I haven't finished which they didn't respond to. They sat me back and then asked me whether I had finished. I shook my head. Now I had to deal with a number of questions, none of which I wanted. (Do you want more time?, Shall we help you?, Do you want your head supported?). I felt a wave of despair flooding me. At the same time I felt cornered by the carers trying to help me. They tried to wipe my mouth, I lashed out with my teeth to keep them at distance. The carer commented, "There is no reason to bite", which gave me a shock because I instantly realised I was presenting challenging behaviour. That made me cry and the carer even more uncomfortable. I realised I had followed a basic animalistic instinct: trying to bite, like a dog, a wasp, or a lion in a cage.

When we talked about it later, the carer told me how difficult it is for them when I scream and not try to communicate calmly. I felt hurt because I had tried exactly that by shaking my head. I would have needed to be asked before they sat me back whether I want to be sat back and the whole situation would have been avoided.

This was written after an incident at lunchtime toileting as an incident report to be filed in my notes and for staff to read.

The Panther, Poem by R. M. Rilke[35]

His vision, from the constantly passing bars,
has grown so weary that it cannot hold
anything else. It seems to him there are
a thousand bars; and behind the bars, no world.

As he paces in cramped circles, over and over,
the movement of his powerful soft strides
is like a ritual dance around a center
in which a mighty will stands paralyzed.

Only at times, the curtain of the pupils
lifts, quietly—. An image enters in,
rushes down through the tensed, arrested muscles,
plunges into the heart and is gone.

---

35   https://www.thereader.org.uk/featured-poem/

Facing the Animal in me*
[25th July 2014]
[Communication with the care agency. In this part the names of the carers have been changed, to protect confidentiality.]

Today the following happened:

Anna and Fiona hoisted me onto the commode. I didn't sit very well, somehow my bottom bones pressed into the chair. I wanted Anna and Fiona to swap because the last two days Anna positioned me on the commode perfectly well on the first attempt. She placed me at a different angle so neither bones nor tissues were squeezed on the commode. I tried to point with my eyes for them to swap, trying to direct Fiona to the hoist and Anna behind me but neither of them understood. They tried to find out by asking questions. The question I needed was not amongst them. They tried to sit me more comfortably with the opposite result. They offered me the typewriter, which I didn't want because my hands are too paralysed to type. The letter board would have solved the problem, but both did not know how to use it. Again I felt desperate. This situation would have been easy to resolve had

I been able to communicate. What I really wished to happen was Anna showing Fiona how she pulls the sling to position me.

Both tried to help me but they could not understand and nothing comforted me. Fiona put her arm in front of me to adjust my position. In this situation in a fraction of a second I bit Fiona strongly into her arm. This happened completely unintendedly and was a shock for me. Her arm got badly bruised with the teeth marks visible.

I was in tears because I had bitten the person, who cares so much for me. I was so shocked because I was not in control. And I know this is not the first incident but it is the worst. Fiona had a shock too of course and the pain and was upset for being treated like that. I had terrible pain because I was the offender and I was unable to communicate.

After the morning care was completed, I tried to let Fiona know that this happened as a reflex and unintendedly. I asked for her forgiveness. But I had to face this as an animalic aspect which is part of me, it is in me. Most of my adult life I could pretend challenging behaviour would never happen.

As a child I have bitten myself when physical or emotional pain became unbearable. Today I cannot do that because I am paralysed. But this animalic instinct to bite the pain away is surfacing in me now. It frightens me deeply, because I realise it could happen again.

Facing the Animal in me*

> *Ute was heartbroken about this event and it took more than a week before her cheerful side began to emerge again. She insisted on having a professional risk assessment of her behaviour from the care agency, even though Fiona did not want to follow through with anything. Afterwards, carers implemented safe ways of moving and handling her without their arms being in reach for her mouth. As far as I know no other similar incident occurred.*

Night routine*

Dear Sarah [not real name] 25/Oct 2014

You do not need to apologise. Your reaction is deeply human. I value your caring attitude and your sense of humour so much.

It is night, there the day consciousness is a bit dimmed. I see it in the increased difficulty to use the word board for you and your colleagues. And how I am at night, you know anyway. Sometimes I struggle to know how I can communicate.

I am always glad to see your face even if I have not called but the noises from my bedroom made you come in. It is reassuring for me that if in doubt you come in and check on me.

I have good nights because I know I am in caring hands by all of you. Thank you.

**[11th December 2014,
direct communication with her carers*]**

Because I have better nights now, I have adapted a technique of not fully waking up when I require assistance. The most likely event is repositioning of the napkin [piece of material used to cover her lips but not the whole face], which has slipped, leaving me with a dry and cold mouth. At night my mouth drops open.

The second likely event is that I get warm and need the duvet folded back to release excess heat.

This is usually done with my bedroom door open using the light from the corridor. All other tasks require the word board and the light from the bedside table. We never used the main lights because that would awaken me fully. Once fully awake, I find it difficult to go back to sleep.

You might find me agitated. This happens when I wake up with pain or with anxiety. I can wake up with anxiety because sometimes I do not know whether I am inside or outside my body. People who are not paralysed move in bed, which helps to feel united with the body. I lose the feeling for my body because I cannot move. I only feel areas of pressure: the soles of my feet, my bottom and nothing else. Therefore I feel like I am in a no-man's land when I wake up. My thinking tells me everything is alright but physical feeling is alarmed because I do not feel my own body.

In the morning I like the heating turned on and the window shut between six and half past six in my bedroom. Otherwise it is too cold for washing and dressing.

Moving, Handling and Touch*
[26th October 2014]

This chapter is about touch and what is called, in care-related jargon, "moving and handling." I am talking only about the handling of *people*, not objects. Being a nurse myself, I have experienced both sides of the subject, first as caregiver, later on the receiving end.

I would like you, the reader, to work together with me. I will ask you to do a few simple daily activities – such as washing your face, putting your trousers on, and the like – and as you do them, I would like you to closely observe *how* you do them. The better you know how you do it yourself, the better you can understand what I am talking about.

Now, in October 2014, I appear very frail and vulnerable in my body. I have lost most of my muscular substance. The disease has affected most of my motoric nerves, destroying them due to overstimulation. A muscle without nerve connection can no longer receive the command for activity and subsequently dies off. Therefore my body appears bony and the skin can be moved in all directions, as it is not firmly connected with the underlying muscular substance. The subcutaneous fat has melted down significantly, though fat still appears to aggregate at the abdomen and thighs. It is no surprise that the staff is worried about hurting me.

I do not see myself. Due to paralysis I can only see what happens to be in front of my eyes. But I perceive myself still as the same person I have always been, and this person is not frail but in the fullness of life. Therefore I do not understand why people are so worried about hurting me. To be more precise: I do understand when I think about it but I can not relate to it with my feelings.

Due to muscular waste the natural position of my limbs' connection with the joints can easily be disrupted. I noticed it in October 2013 when I received, for the first time in my life, personal care [*in the rehab care home, where Ute stayed for one month, as an emergency solution before she could move into her final home in Brookthorpe*]. I had slide sheets which were kept in bed all night, so staff did not need to roll my body with their hands. I noticed their complete absence of knowledge on how to use slide sheets. I had to teach all my carers how to use them. I met only one Reablement worker who preemptively knew how to use them and who worked with them according to standard. This lady had worked alongside the physiotherapist for years.

Besides her, other staff members told me rolling the body without using sheets is faster and holding the client with their hand in position is more secure. I noticed in using this technique my spine got pulled in different directions because hips and shoulders were moved at different degrees or my legs were forgotten and dragged my hip back. I was not at all stable because the legs were not put in a recovery position. And the carers are quite right: they had to hold my body because it was not stable. But holding my body on its side for washing my back while the legs are dragging it back is painful for both my carers and myself. The carers will inevitably suffer from lower-back pain sooner or later when using such 'technique'.

In my view, that is the beauty of using slide sheets and a recovery position, that one can avoid pain and damage for both carer and client. I found myself making step-by-step drawings to explain how to turn me into a recovery position, using 'Wendy Lett' slide sheets. My previous experience as a moving and handling trainer came in quite handy.

My knees get hurt when overstretched. This happens when I lie on my back and the staff lift my leg at the foot [instead of supporting it under the knee joint] for example to pull trousers up or down or to wash my legs. As long as I could still speak I often had to say "bend my legs".

Observe yourself: how do you dress your bottom half?

Exactly, you bend your leg at the knee and hip. Only under care conditions do legs get overstretched during dressing. We see our clients showing signs of pain in personal care due to poor moving and handling. Staff is tempted to request pain-relieving medication rather than reviewing their moving and handling techniques.

Dear reader, if you are a carer, I can only recommend trying it out so you experience in your own body how it feels when what I am talking about happens. Lie on your back and ask a partner to lift your leg at the foot as long as it normally takes to dress the bottom half. Observe what it feels like. Then do the same again but bend the knee and observe the difference.

The other painful move was to move my legs to the side. Because the muscles at my hips were almost gone, it felt as if the leg would move out of the socket at hip level. In this case the leg acts as a lever, which aggravates the impact on the hip joint. I think this is a typical MND-related problem that people with other types of paralysis might not have. But the problem with the overstretched leg [is most likely an] experience of the average care-dependent client.

While in the beginning of my care dependency, it was only my legs and hips that appeared to be vulnerable, this extended to shoulder and arms soon after. Again I could and still can tolerate all forwards and upwards movements of my arms, but I am in pain with all movements to the side because it affects my shoulder joints. My arm acts as a lever. Particularly, when carers use the elbow as a grab handle, I can not tolerate the pain. I did put a note up: "Don't use my elbow as a grab handle!" But I also had to teach staff how to move my arms during personal care [without causing me pain]. This was fine as long as I could talk, but got increasingly difficult after my speech had gone. I started to scream, to shout – I got agitated because I was afraid one of their next actions would hurt me.

Moving, Handling and Touch*

I admit I gave my carers a hard time with my fear-driven behaviour. But I had reasons to be frightened, for example, when staff tried to raise the headrest in my bed while I was lying on my side. Raising my head with my body in a side position would have put my spine at risk. In this case, my previously being a moving and handling trainer did not exactly help my anxiety, because I was aware of what could go wrong whilst my carers were not.

I describe these moving and handling issues not because I think my carers were not good enough. They all did the best they could do for me. What I question is the quality of the moving and handling *training*, which all care professionals have to attend once a year. If this is the outcome, the training is a waste of time and money. It is not sufficient to show a video of what to do and what not to do and let them sit in the hoist. The correct moving and handling needs to be practised often enough by all carers involved in the care of bed-ridden clients, so it becomes part of every care routine. Just demonstrating how to do it or showing a video demonstration clearly does not achieve the same result.

The physiotherapist and the OT came out to assess positioning at night and the use of pillows as positioning aids. I had only one carer at night. Turning with slide sheets by only one person is possible but requires good technique. Pulling me up in the bed is not safely possible for one person, so I got two dedicated carers allocated, who covered most of my nights. But my sleep became more and more disrupted. I could no longer tolerate the side-sleeping position I had used for so many years, I could not communicate, because my speech deteriorated and, on top of all that, I started menopause and got hot flushes. I tried to communicate verbally and my carers tried to guess what I was saying, but that got more difficult. I got agitated because I was frightened by not being able to communicate when I had physical needs which needed addressing.

Now I sleep on my back all night. Major positioning is no longer needed, because today, my arms are almost fully paralysed. That means I can no longer position them as needed, when I am turned into a recovery position. As a result they might end up under my body if staff are not aware of it. When carers position me onto my back, my trunk flips over like a bag of potatoes, my arm is left on the side or gets stuck on my chest – that especially happens when it is wet from washing, because people concentrate to get my leg right and forget about the arm and head. I found a video online that addressed some of these issues and showed my carers, but it would have been better if they had known the right techniques ahead of time.

Touch*
[written for the book Oct/Nov 2014]

This is an interesting subject that is closely related to the culture we grew up with. We can discern functional touch and social touch. In care provision touch is functional. Positioning, washing, dressing, and transferring are the main areas of touch. Before I go into details, observe yourself. How do you wash your face? Take a few minutes to get a clear picture or try it out.

I have the following observations: People try to wash my face as follows: first, wipe with the flannel carefully from the forehead to the chin around the face, first one side then the other, next they carefully wipe my eyes, then nose, then mouth. Some people repeat the whole procedure a second time.

How did you wash your face? Exactly, in one go over the whole face. Did you ever try to wash your face the way I just described?

Next task: dry the face. Think for a moment: what do you do to dry your face?

How did you dry your face? How do you grab the towel, with one or both hands? I can tell you how I used to do it. I took the towel with both hands and rubbed my face until it was dry. And that is what I expect my carers to do because I want to be dry.

Now, I tell you what I experience: People take the towel in one hand, trying to dry by carefully wiping around the outside of my face, then carefully touching my eyes with the towel, then going with the same technique over my nose, mouth and cheeks.

I could continue with the whole body. Well, my body is not dirty, so it does not matter. But think of your private parts – how do you wash them? Sometimes I do not feel clean, because my private parts are not washed thoroughly.

I noticed cultural differences between English and foreign carers. The English try to avoid touch as much as possible, while the foreign care staff is more likely to touch my body and wash and dry it more thoroughly.

Last element of touch is moving my body or parts of my body. Usually people are very careful because they do not want to hurt me. Before I tell you my experience, a little exercise: lift your stretched arm as slowly as possible. You can do that in a standing position or lying in bed. Keep your arm stretched while you are doing it, and do it as slowly as you can. What do you feel? What does your arm feel like?

That is exactly how it feels for me if you carefully and slowly lift my arm because I have full body sensation. The reason for this is again because the arm acts as a lever. The same applies for legs or back. The back I find particularly tricky because I have no balance. To be held in an unstable position while someone puts my vest into my trousers or a pillow in my back is challenging and can be painful.

The hoist: the hoist is one of these wonderful apparatus that make care work bearable because the hoist does the lifting. There are various hoists on the market, and for each hoist there are different types of slings, usually in three different sizes. Widely used are the toilet sling (access sling) and the full-body sling. My hoist was ordered by the OT a month before I actually needed it. But there was the question of what sling would be suitable. I got a full-body sling, but being continent I continue to use the toilet. This requires a toilet sling. The toilet sling for the type of hoist I am using is not suitable for me because it catches the weight of the body under the arms. This can not work because arms and shoulders are weak due to muscular waste. The sling that the OT of the supplying company thought should work proved not to be the right one, so to find out what is on the market apart from the standard slings, we booked an assessment with the supplier.

I wanted a toilet sling. I discovered a toilet sling when I worked at the nursing home, which does not transfer weight to arms and shoulders. I needed to persuade both OTs to try it. Sure enough the sling fitted perfectly. When I started using the hoist it turned out none of my carers had seen this sling before, but all of them loved it because it did not put strain on my shoulders and arms. My OT considered this sling to be suitable for a number of clients but the local supplier did not have it in stock.

Why is it that people do not know about improved equipment? Because it is more expensive than standard equipment?

Itch*
[written for the book, Oct/Nov 2014]

Do you ever think about what you do when something itches? I assume the first thing you do is go there with your hand. If it is an insect you shy it away; if it is a hair, you wipe it out of your face. If the itch continues you might rub, scratch, apply cream or ignore it.

When I have an itch I need to ask for help. There the trouble begins. How do I describe where the itch is when I can not see it and when I can not check it out with my hand? Recently I woke up with a terrible itch and believed it was on my forehead. I called the carer, and spelled out on the word board as well as I could that I wanted my forehead wiped with the towel. Now the carer wiped carefully from one side to the middle of the forehead then from the other side to the middle of the forehead. I realised then that the itch was not on my forehead but somewhere between forehead and eyes. It would take too long to describe all the steps needed to get the carer to rub firmly the whole region between my eyes.

Living a fulfilled life with MND*
[November 2014]
[Ute wrote this in preparation for a training session for local hospice staff. At the beginning of the session, this paper was read out. Ute answered questions at the end.]

My name is Ute. I am here today with Christina, my carer. I live on my own in a bungalow assisted by a substantial care package. I am CHC [Continuous Health Care] funded since January 2014. I have two carers doing waking nights and one carer during the day. A second carer visits four times a day for personal care and toileting. My carers are my muscles. I cannot do anything for myself independently.

I have a strong network of family, friends and carers who contribute to my social life and give me the ability to carry on with all my study groups, activities and projects.

I was diagnosed with MND in July 2011 but had already figured out what I had around Christmas 2010, because I observed fasciculations in my legs and lower back, affecting one or two segments of a spinal nerve. This and the absence of pain convinced me it must be a neuromuscular condition, of which, in my view, the worst one I knew was MND. I had a number of worried nights, lying awake and observing my body carefully. Particularly worrying was a kind of 'noise' in my body, something like a high-pitch vibration, that created a constant background of vibration.

At that time I had a considerable foot drop and a weak right ankle, which caused me to fall frequently. Nothing to play with, this was serious, and I knew it.

The process of getting diagnosed took a year from my first appointment with the osteopath to the delivery of the death sentence by the neurologist. I did not speed this process up because I needed time to get ready for the news and particularly ready to deal with the reaction of my environment.

I got all kinds of reactions from disbelief and shock to anger and wanting me to fight it. I was bombarded with recommendations for medicine, treatment, doctors, healers, in half of Europe and America. People wanted me to take action on all of their recommendations, which I did not do. I wanted to get on with my life. My sister helped spread the news. That was a great help because I got tired of always telling the same sad news and that did me no good.

I can discern four different stages of living with the condition:

1. Pre-diagnosis: first symptoms, which did not make any sense, then growing insight something is not right, later significant impairment due to foot drop and weakness of right ankle (2009–2011).

2. Post diagnosis: I continued to work, but my employers and I had to adapt gradually to my increasing disability (2011–2013).
3. Massive skill loss that could not be compensated anymore, leaving me fully paralysed and without verbal communication (October 2013-2014).
4. Rock bottom: major deterioration completed, less energy required for adaptation, life became more important again (since September 2014).

Now I have reached a steady stage. I know there is more to come when breathing will be affected and my swallowing can deteriorate further. I might need suction and perhaps a tracheotomy[36] or a ventilator, I don't know yet, but it is likely.

I take homoeopathic medication, which my sister prepares and discusses on my behalf with the prescribing doctor [in Germany]. It stopped the development of breathing symptoms in March.

> *March 2014. Ute stated in several conversations that she first observed breathing problems in November 2013, which resolved when she started taking the homoeopathic remedies again in late November, from then on with assistance, which she had stopped taking when she could no longer self administer. It is surprising to me that she wrote "March" here because she also shared that the breathing symptoms disappeared within a week or two of starting the homoeopathic remedies again.*

---

36 tracheotomy is a surgical procedure which involves creating a direct airway incision made on the trachea

I take Movicol for regular bowel movement and Atropine one drop four times a day to stop hypersalivation. I have paracetamol at home for use as needed.

The losses that impacted most on my life are the loss of voice and speech. I started to lose my singing voice in July 2013. In September my speaking voice broke, dropped in pitch and felt no longer like mine. My capacity to articulate words began to deteriorate the year before. My lip seal broke, which had negative effects on both articulation and eating. I started to become a messy eater. Last year in October I had to think about what I wanted to say because certain words such as museum I could no longer pronounce – I could no longer put my lips tight enough together to form the M. My speech got slurred; less and less was understandable. My eating got worse, I coughed a lot on food, food dropped out of my mouth, I accidentally bit my tongue, cheeks and lips. This was highly frustrating. I perceived myself no longer as human when it came to eating. I started to burp in order to get rid of the air I had swallowed. It felt more like animal behaviour and it was a huge challenge because of my need for dignity.

"..." [This omitted section is already discussed in previous chapters.]

Luckily, I had made an early decision in favour of eye-gaze equipment and my Speech Therapist had requested an assessment, well ahead of point of need. We both expected a rapid paralysation of my whole body. My fabulous speech therapist got the representative from the local software-supplying company to bring the eye-gaze equipment and do an assessment, which was successful. She asked the MND society to provide an eye-gaze camera on loan. Literally on the day I could no longer use the mouse, I got my whole eye-gaze equipment sorted. Writing, talking and operating the computer I now do with my eyes.

The two main contributing factors helping me to achieve that in time were:

1. Anticipation of what my needs might realistically be in approximately six months' time.
2. A proactive SALT [Speech And Language Team] team, acting well ahead of the point of need and not waiting until the need occurred. The waiting time even being on top of the waiting list would have left me possibly for several weeks unable to communicate. I know I am exceptionally lucky; the reality for many clients is different. The same applies for the PEG [feeding tube into the stomach].

I made an early decision pro PEG because I did not want to die of starvation. This was not difficult for me to do because, as a nurse, I know how the PEG works. And I know that it does not extend life but contributes to life quality. I started to use the PEG three months ago when my eating caused so much coughing and carried a high risk of my suffocating on food, if it went down the wrong way. At that time I could not clear my throat, I needed clapping on my back. The whole situation was frightening. So I announced my decision to stop eating. I had to wait for two more weeks until enough of my carers had received PEG training. Not eating has improved my quality of life enormously.

With Christina in front of the house under the cherry tree
[not part of the report]

I know of one person living with MND who died of starvation. Her speech was terribly slurred and all that could be understood when she tried to speak was her talking about food near the end of her life. I know of another person suffering with Parkinson's disease who was begging for food. Staff refused because his swallowing was not safe. His daughter felt awful about how he died.

This touches on a controversial subject. End of life. I am an end-of-life patient. Quite a lot of my friends and professionals did expect me to be dead by now due to my rapid deterioration earlier this year. I was expected to sign a DNR [Do Not Resuscitate] form and state that I want to be treated

Living a fulfilled life with MND*

at home and not be admitted to hospital. I refused, because of course I want to be treated in hospital like everybody else, should that be required. So far I have not even had a chest infection. I consider myself a perfectly healthy person, living with a life-limiting condition. I need to be healthy in order to put up with MND.

So far my report. Are there any questions? Christina will help me with the word board. [Because of the time that takes] I can only answer with a few words spelled on the word board. Doing this session today is an interesting experiment and intentionally so, because this is the reality of communication for many people with this and similar illnesses. It is neither in my, nor probably in your, comfort zone. Let's see how far we get.

For further questions I would suggest putting them in writing. I will write my answer and email to the hospice for forwarding it to the participants.

Thank you for listening. Ute

[*The questions and comments that came back are not available at this point in time in 2024.*]

The benefits of the MND Society*
[9th October 2014]

[This was prepared for a fundraising event in Ute's garden, the ice-bucket challenge, where sponsored volunteers would have a bucket of water with ice cubes poured over them.]

The MND Society is a charity supporting people living with MND (Motor Neuron Disease). The money they raise is used to supply equipment, initiating and financing research in the causes and treatment of MND, to fast tract patients with MND in the health system, so that they do not die before they have reached the top of the waiting list. They support patients as well as their carers to deal with the impact that MND has on their lives.

The MND Society keeps an eye on the availability and quality of services provided for people living with MND. At the moment [Oct 2014] we have 52 people diagnosed with MND in Gloucestershire, [approximate population in the UK at the time ca 62'000'000] which shows the disease is, compared to the majority of common diseases, relatively rare.

I benefited from the health visitor to discuss my options before I had to ask for care. Zambodhi had a number of meetings with one of their [MND Society's] volunteers.

I have equipment, which is supported by the MND Society. First of all, the wheelchair. In Gloucestershire they supply two powered wheelchairs with a high level of support to ensure people living with MND get a wheelchair at the point of need and not only when they have moved sufficiently up the waiting list. With this support they ensure the right type of wheelchair is supplied while the person is still alive.

This is similar with eye-gaze equipment. People like me are eligible to have eye-gaze equipment on the NHS. But it takes about six months before one even gets an appointment for the assessment. Then the camera and screen have to be ordered and God only knows how much more waiting time would pass before the equipment would be supplied. In my case the local speech and language therapist visited when my speech deteriorated and supplied me with various equipment for a trial period. Out of that I got the light writer. Because it was already obvious that I would soon lose control of my hands, we considered the eye gaze and the assessment with the Bristol based Speech and Language department was requested, way ahead of my point of need. I tried the eye gaze in May. Camera and screen were supplied by the software provider for initial assessment. At the end of June I got a camera and screen from the Bristol Speech and Language team. The camera was lent by the MND Society for the duration, until

The benefits of the MND Society*

the camera ordered for me arrived. The screen I am using is the property of the MND Society on loan.

You know how important communication is for me. Thanks to the MND Society and the marvellous interdisciplinary professional team, I got major pieces of equipment at the point of need. Therefore I am more than happy to host the Ice Bucket Challenge. The proceedings of this event are obviously in favour of the MND Society.

> Ute's carer, Lianne, and the Manager of the Care Agency, Denise, both volunteered for having a bucket of water and ice cubes poured over their heads. The event took place in Ute's garden on a nice warm October day and raised £300 for the MND Society.

Lianne on the left and Denise right of Ute volunteering for the ice bucket challenge (right)

Putting the House in Order*
[28th September 2014]

I don't know how much time I have left. Even now, there are fewer and fewer things that I can do. Teaching is difficult, because I cannot speak and to do it in writing cannot replace the spoken word.

What are my tasks in this world?

I enjoy it most when I can contribute to somebody else making their next step in life. How things are for me now is more like pulling the strings in the background. This is with full awareness of where I get my inspiration from.

There is on the one hand the inspiration coming from individualities who are currently not incarnated, the so-called dead. This happens spontaneously and is depending on who is present in my home. Sometimes I notice the presence of an individuality on the spiritual side of existence, who was either known to myself or to the person visiting me. Usually we are talking about this person or an event they were involved in. I become aware of their supersensible presence. On most occasions I let my visitor know who is with us.

Often I feel a message coming through. This is completely without words; it is rather a sensing within myself. Within me I know what the so-called dead want us to know. Often there is a feeling that goes along with it. This I sense deeply inside me. That is so intense that it brings tears to my eyes. This seems to be the feeling of the individual present, rather than my own feeling.

When my brother and my mum visited in January [2014], the following happened: We were talking about our family of origin and suddenly I became aware of the presence of my father's mother, who had died in 1990. Mum was just talking about the fact that she didn't feel accepted by her mother-in-law. I became aware of the presence of her mother in law, my paternal grandmother, which felt heavy as if covered in a cloud of sadness so that I started to cry. I was completely aware this was not my own sadness. I felt rather neutral although I was expressing her utter sadness. I told my mother and brother who were present. I am not sure how far that registered with mum because she was occupied with her own story but it certainly did with my brother. While our mother told us how she felt disregarded by her 'in-laws', my grandmother's sadness increased and I felt her pleading for forgiveness. So I asked mum if she would forgive her mother-in-law. Mum responded by saying "This happened long ago, that is anyway forgiven." My granny didn't seem to feel any relief; the sadness I experienced as hers was as heavy as before. I pointed out to mum that her mother in law is here asking her whether she can forgive her. Now mum replied with a clear 'yes'. Instantly I felt a heavy burden fall off my granny. Her presence felt light in both senses of the word. It was similar to jumping in the air with delight. I felt her smiling and becoming light with relief.

We talked about what happened a bit more but moved on to other subjects relatively soon. The presence of my granny faded away but the important bit, the reconciliation between our mum and her mother in law, our granny, had taken place.

In this case I was only the transmitter of a process between two people, one of them incarnated and sitting in my living room, the other in their spiritual existence.

It is a different situation when I become aware that my action is directly inspired by a person who is not incarnated. The first time that ever happened to me was ten years ago during my work as district nurse in Luxembourg. We had a lady in her nineties who lived most of her life with extensive leg ulcers in both legs. One day after three years of knowing her she told me the story of the open wounds on her legs which backdated until 1944 during the German occupation of Luxembourg. One day her husband didn't return from work in the nearby town. She stayed up all night waiting for him to come home but he didn't come. She stayed awake the following night the night after but no sign of him. She stayed awake most of the night in the following weeks and slept little in months to come. During the day she looked after their two children and their small holding and at night she was waiting for her husband.

Finding Connection and Fulfillment in the Face of Motor Neuron Disease

After six months of waiting a compassionate soul told her what had happened to her husband. The Germans raided the local trade-union office to get hold of the local union activist. They couldn't find the person they were after. So they grabbed the first person they could get hold of – her husband – and tortured him to death. They tied him behind a car and dragged him through the whole town to show the local population what would happen to them if they did not cooperate. It was so cruel that for six months nobody had dared to tell his wife about it. During the time she was waiting for him her leg ulcers developed.

I felt very honoured that she told me the whole story eventually even though I am German. Only a few months later she got weaker and didn't feel well. She was admitted to hospital but her condition didn't improve. Eventually she was discharged to die at home. Surprisingly though, her ulcers got better day by day while she was growing ever weaker. It was obvious that she was preparing for death.

As a German citizen, albeit born 13 years after the war, I felt the need to ask her for forgiveness [on behalf of that generation of my people] for the murder of her husband. For a long time I didn't dare to do it. As she became so frail that we expected her to die soon, the need to ask for forgiveness became urgent but I didn't find the right moment. Either the family was present or a colleague with whom I could not imagine sharing such a delicate question. On the day of her death, I saw her four times. I got the golden opportunity in the morning. She was lucid, wanted to use the commode

Putting the House in Order*

and was up for a chat. I spent half an hour with her on my own with the question burning in my mind but did not dare to ask. I was far too frightened to do that. She died the same afternoon without my being offered the chance for reconciliation.

At the time, I was unaware that reconciliation might be as important for her as it would be for the soul who was nagging me to ask for it. With my today's consciousness I would trust the signs and ask. The client was fully conscious, and I was on my own with her – that shows the field is prepared. And if the field is prepared in such an obvious manner, then no doubt asking her for forgiveness would have been the right thing to do.

Since I became paralysed I experience and recognise such situations more frequently. It does not frighten me any more. But what I do not know is, how many more occasions there are, which I overlook. I am sometimes aware of spiritual beings, although I cannot see them. And I do not know who is present. But again I sometimes know why they are there.

This might be part of my new task to share these events with the people present in my home or simply transmit messages to the persons concerned. I learnt that the physical impression I have of my fellow human beings is completely different from how I would perceive them in their spiritual reality to say the least. For example, let me tell you a story of when I talked to a person whom I perceived as weak and unable to show leadership in life, since he had lost all his inherited property. When he reached out to me from the spiritual realm, he revealed the motive for his action: pure love. This person has sacrificed his own life plans in favour of his father's needs, a deed which was never recognised in his entire life.

One day in advent last year, mysterious events of a kind I never believed in when I heard other people talking about such things, happened in my house. At midday a picture fell in front of my eyes slowly off the wall. The frame disintegrated and went into pieces. Neither the glass nor the picture itself got damaged. It was completely still; I could not observe any outer trigger for the picture to come off the wall. In the afternoon of the same day I sat with a visitor in the living room involved in small talk. (At that time I could still talk.) Suddenly I saw a vase with flowers, which had been standing on the floor for more than a week, slowly tipping over. I watched it happening but from the wheelchair I could do nothing about it. At that point I started thinking that this is rather strange; it was the second time that something happened in front of my eyes without any obvious reason. My visitor had to deal with the water on the floor and to rearrange the flowers.

Towards the evening the weather changed. It started to rain accompanied by a blustery wind, howling on the windows. I felt quite comfortable in my cosy sitting room, listening to the elements outside. Suddenly I became aware of the sound of dripping water. I checked the kitchen but all the taps were closed. It seemed to be in the living room. I saw water dripping into a vase with flowers which stood on

Putting the House in Order*

the mantelpiece. Each falling drop landed with a splash in the vase. The water was dripping from the ceiling close to the chimney. This was the obvious place to expect a leak, given the weather. At that point I realised something is trying to draw my attention.

I did a meditation, in which I acknowledged that something wanted my attention. As soon as I had done so, the dripping stopped. What did not stop was the rain outside. It continued as heavy as before for several more hours. There I sat knowing someone wanted my attention and did not know how to find out who it was. So I meditated on the events in the evenings before I went to sleep. After two or three days, I woke up with a picture of the derelict barn of the farm where I did my apprenticeship. Then I knew who was asking for attention, but I still wondered why.

The answer to that came a few weeks later. A friend visited who many years ago had done her apprenticeship together with me at the same farm in Carinthia. While we were warming old memories, the person who had owned the farm was with us, the person who had been trying to get my attention all this time. Being aware of him now, I got the impression he had not even tried to follow his life plans because of the duty placed on him by his father [to carry on working as a biodynamic farmer and developing the farm]. His father had passed the whole estate on to this son.

Now while he was present, I felt he had sacrificed his plans to serve his father's wishes. And because he tried to fulfil his father's intentions, which resulted in not being able

167

to realise his own, the farm did struggle economically under his leadership. In the end the whole estate was lost, the huge stable, which was the largest in Carinthia and the pride of the couple who built it about 100 years ago, fell into ruins and needed to be pulled down. All the people working and learning on the farm had left. For many years the once proud estate lay dilapidated and empty.

The last remaining person there was the owner [the son who had taken on the farm] who died in 2005 of cancer. We, the apprentices on the farm [at the time], perceived him as 'light weight', as someone who runs a farm without being a farmer himself. The farm was run in such a way that it created a huge deficit year after year. None of us saw his merits in helping the biodynamic agriculture movement in Austria come off the ground nor [did we appreciate] his involvement in agriculture related politics. The economic disaster developing on his own farm had blocked my view of all his achievements. And here he was wanting recognition for what he had done.

My friend and I talked about his life from the point of him taking on his father's work. We previously understood his life out of what he had not achieved rather than out of what he did achieve, but now we had a fuller picture. From the point of view of spiritual development, recognition of achievements are important because they provide the strength needed to face the shortcomings of life on earth after death. From this perspective the always positive obituaries make sense: they help the deceased to look back on their life with the strengthening power of their achievements.

I still have the feeling my work with him is not completed because there is not a positive outcome. It would not surprise me if there were more communications.

My experience with Meditation*
[28th November 2014]

My attempts to meditate are full of obstacles. I cannot close my eyes when I want to. Therefore, I try to meditate at night in bed, but in a lying position I cannot focus my thoughts as I want to. It is a constant struggle. Usually, I am not able to do the Lord's Prayer to the end. I tried with the meditation (I used to do regularly), but the same result. I have a long-standing practice of prayer, which I used to do twice a day. At the moment, I manage only once a day, at night. Each time I wake up, I start where I left off last time [where I fell asleep].

My sleep is less disrupted now, and I have dreams again. Sometimes I get sudden clarity about questions I am living with. In this respect, my nights are quite productive. During the day, my meditative work has stopped because of [needing] the computer. I spend hours every day for my daily communication and writing work.

Being in a paralysed body, I have weird experiences. I find myself above my body, not able to get in but also unable to remain outside it. I know I should be in there, but I do not know how to get in because my body appears to resist. This is rather frightening. I observe the will activity in my body. This becomes apparent because the will is trapped in the paralysed body. The full will energy, which is strong enough to get a body in motion, is trapped. It transforms [itself] in[to] warmth and emotions.

My way forward: carrying on, to show up [try again and again]. This is all I can do. At some point, there will be a result. I do not need to know [now] what that [will be].

Review of the Year 2014*
[Nov/Dec 2014]

Dear friends,

This is the first review I am writing with my eyes. I look back on a year that brought massive, yet expected, changes. I've lost my speech, stopped eating and am almost completely paralysed. I live alone with 24/7 care. My carers replace my muscles. Without their help I can do nothing; with their help I can do an amazing lot of things.

As long as I experienced the massive progression of paralysis, it was difficult for me to adjust to the process because I had to give up something else almost every day. And some things are so deeply connected to my personality, that I felt my dignity as a human being was violated.

Due to the loss of my lip muscles, I can no longer speak. Only with great effort can I (barely) drink, and before I lost the ability to eat, I was only able to still do it with a great deal of mess. Food and saliva kept dripping from my mouth, which was particularly unpleasant. The process of completely losing my speech dragged on for more than half a year. I have always known that my greatest challenge would be the loss of verbal communication, as I have seen with my father-in-law [who had Parkinson's Disease] and some patients in my care and the prospect of it frightened me. This has happened to me now – only with the lucky difference that I can fall back on computer-aided communication.

Now that I am more or less completely paralysed, the problem of the progression of my disease seems the smallest problem of all, because there is no noticeable change to me any more and it is therefore possible for me to adjust to living in a paralysed body. Only at night does it sometimes give me problems, when I wake up and experience myself outside of my body and don't know how to get back in.

In August I stopped eating because I got too much food nearly into my windpipe. This led to frightening situations, with thick mucus in my airways that I couldn't cough up. Therefore it wasn't difficult for me to say goodbye to food, I know how much quality of life I gained through it. Today, four times a day, I get vanilla-flavoured tube feedings injected directly into my stomach through the PEG. We toasted with it on my birthday. It tastes awful but luckily I don't have to taste it.

After all the losses, what is the gain?

A greater spiritual permeability for sure, both in my body and in my environment. In my body I observe my will. It is trapped inside my body because the body can no longer convert will impulses into action. The will energy is constantly crashing against my paralysed limbs. According to the law of conservation of energy, it does not simply disappear but is transformed into emotions and warmth. Here a wide field of inner observation opens up to me.

I now have new experiences in my immediate environment. Sometimes the deceased are present. That doesn't happen because it is so beautiful but because there is work to be done. Mostly this is about unfinished business between people, which now weighs heavily because for the dead there is no physical body that could carry out what needs to be done. I have, on a number of occasions, felt the relief of those who have died, whose requests have been heard and granted. Now that sounds pretty esoteric, but feels normal to me after the initial shock.

I stopped [my administrative nursing job] in April, because I could no longer use the computer keyboard. By that time I could also no longer speak. I didn't experience the loss of work as drastic, it was just time to turn to other things. After two difficult months of transition, I got my eye-gaze-computer tool, which enables me to write by reading the movements of my eyes. With this I feel again as part of the discourse in society as a whole.

Because I can only 'speak' when I am at the computer, I write a lot. I sometimes write documents for the farm that require research and take on other occasional tasks. That and multiple requests from many directions has finally persuaded me to write a book about my experiences. I am in the rare position of being on both sides of the fence at the same time: patient here, nurse there. That is how I write my book, as soon as I feel inspired about a topic [rather than along the timeline]. Besides that I follow my interests like observing nature, the stars, reading, farming and more.

Recently I have acquired a new field of activity: public relations in living with MND. Here in England people think that the life I lead must be just miserable and that I should be spared the experience if possible. Therefore, members of the professional team that accompanies and organises my care urged me to have an advance directive, excluding resuscitation and treatment in hospital. Of course I did not do that, on the grounds that if Stephen Hawking had signed it, he would have been dead for 30 years.

It all started when I made a contribution to an event about the end of life care with MND where we had a good laugh. It became clear to me that people in my situation inevitably end up in a corner of life, considered to be unworthy of living. The general advice is telling me, the latter stages of my illness are no use anyway and better to be without. People asking me why I would want to be treated in hospital, make it just harder for me to experience meaningfulness in my life with terminal illness.

I would like to raise my voice against this fatalism. Too much is fear-driven behaviour, which then makes people travel to Switzerland[37] because they are afraid of the unreasonable demands of the disease. In January 2014 I was classified as 'palliative' with a prospect of imminent death (within three months). That was a bit early for me.

---

37   [to end their lives before their illness takes it, with assistance from agencies equipped to offer physician-assisted suicide to people with terminal illness, which is legal in Switzerland]

Review of the Year 2014*

What keeps me alive? First of all my social context, my friends, study groups, all the inquiries I get, all the people who don't shy away from spending time with me – even though I'm dripping saliva onto my bib, cannot speak and lose my nerve when I am unable to express myself. Also the fact that there are still enough fields of activity there for me and that I see and hear something new every day. I have a sense that my tasks on earth are not yet completed, although I do not know exactly what these tasks consist of. But I trust I will get the time I need. That may sound naive, but nevertheless I trust it will be so.

What awaits me next year after this year has brought physical deterioration? It cannot get much worse, can it? And do I have to go through everything? Stop drinking, congested airways, ventilation? Whilst I knew with certainty that this year that I would have to give up speaking, food and independent body movement, I am not sure at all what the next year has in store for me. I have the impression that I have arrived at the bottom of the 'anthroposophical bathtub[38] or, to put it another way, in Theory U[39] at the bottom of the U. Up until then it was going downhill, now it's going up again.

In other words, the way to the bottom was the preparation of new skills that now need to be developed and consolidated. Accordingly, next year will probably bring a lot of new things. We will see. I am definitely optimistic.

Many greetings, Ute

---

38 Ute's joking reference to coming to such a low place that things can only improve from there.
39 Theory U: Leading from the Future as It Emerges, by Otto Scharmer 2009

Facing death*
[worked on between 3rd and
15th January 2015 in hospital]

A few days before Christmas [2014], I got a cold. I had a sore throat and did not feel well. On the morning of Christmas Eve, I asked [my carers] to call the doctor, who visited and prescribed antibiotics. I took the first lot in the early afternoon, but despite the medication, I deteriorated further. When I was hoisted onto the toilet in the afternoon, my carers observed my lips turning blue. I checked the colour of my fingernails and connected it with the feeling of anxiety. I realised I was lacking oxygen. That meant I no longer had a chance at surviving at home.

I wrote on the screen for my carer to call the ambulance for admission to hospital. I was relieved when they turned up and supplied me with [nasal] oxygen, put me on a stretcher, and took me to A & E[40] at Gloucester Royal Hospital. There, I was put in a hospital bed with oxygen and monitoring of

---

40 Accident and Emergency Department of the hospital

my oxygen saturation[41]. Not the Christmas I would have wished for, but the only chance to survive.

I ruined Christmas Eve for all my friends who wanted to share it with me, but that wasn't the worst thing, by far – the battle for my life had begun, and I quickly got weaker. On Christmas Day, I was transferred from the Acute Care Unit to the Neurology Ward. They treated me very attentively, but I deteriorated further and the oxygen mask was no longer sufficient. The decision was made to put me on a BiPAP mask (an oxygen mask that pumps the oxygen into my body via nose and mouth) and to transfer me to the Respiratory Ward. It was too much for my consciousness to remember the sequence of events from there, because I was fighting against death. Luckily, I had the help of modern medicine – the BiPAP mask was blowing air into my lungs, making them inflate and opening the chest area.

The carer who was with me when my sats dropped and the alarm was raised told me later how impressive it was to see my chest rise as soon as the air of the respirator came in.

Normally, there is a negative pressure that makes lungs take in air. This has to do with the movement of the diaphragm; as the diaphragm moves down, negative pressure in the chest area increases, which triggers the lungs to suck in air again. The air is pushed out when the diaphragm moves up. The respirator, in contrast, produces a *positive* pressure, making the lungs inflate by blowing air in. This is a completely unnatural process, which the body and mind tend

---

41   Oxygen saturation, later abbreviated sats

to resist. This happened to me as well. While the respirator was saving my life, I was fighting the respirator. To make the whole system work, the mask through which the air comes in has to seal the whole nose and mouth area[42]. This already creates a claustrophobic feeling. Now the additional stress factor is the air coming in with positive pressure, because it has not only to inflate the lungs but also to widen the intercostal muscles and push the diaphragm down. The normal process is that the diaphragm pushes the air out, making the thoracic muscles contract for the typical appearance of the exhale.

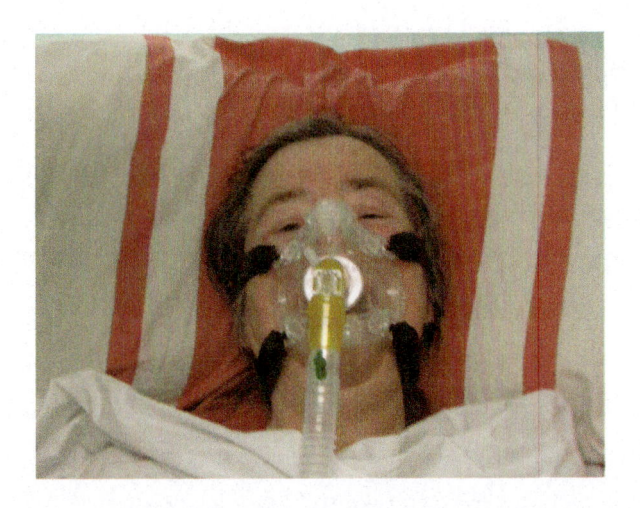

This is, roughly speaking, the mechanical side of the breathing process. The whole breathing process is far more complicated. I mention the mechanical aspect because it is the aspect affected by the disease. MND progressively paralyses

---

42   The mask is strapped very tightly, pressing onto the face so that no gaps occur to let air escape

the diaphragm, which weakens the mechanics of breathing. In my case, the whole fragile process collapsed with the pneumonia I had developed when I was admitted to hospital.

I wanted the staff to take the mask off because I felt overwhelmed by the incoming flow of air. With the mask, I had the feeling I could not breathe, even though the opposite was the case. I remember being quite forceful about it. I was convinced the oxygen, administered through the nose, which I had before was sufficient enough. But even though [I needed] to combat pneumonia, it needed a team and some cruelty to get me on the BiPAP.

In the hospital I was treated with intravenous Antibiotics. The BiPAP secured my actual survival. I got x-rayed and had blood samples taken regularly. I was also given Ranitidine to protect my stomach against stress. Saturation of oxygen, blood pressure, temperature, respiration rate, and blood gases were monitored closely. While that was going on, I faced my inner battle—I felt invaded by the air blown into my chest, and faced endless anxiety with the breathing I could not control.

During the first night on the BiPAP, I concentrated on getting rid of the respirator. I spelled it out on the word board, over and over, to take the mask away. I was convinced the nasal oxygen tube alone would do, without the BiPAP. I do not know how I came across to the hospital staff but certainly not fully *compos mentis*[43].

My consciousness could no longer cope. I decided all of this must be a bad dream, but on the other hand I kept

---

43 having full control of one's mind

Facing death*

thinking this must be real; I was really in hospital, and the carer who was with me showed me it was real. I was thrown to and fro between these poles. At some point I went to sleep for a while. As soon as I woke up, the same battle of consciousness started again. Toward morning, I got calmer because the dream consciousness took over for a while, but as soon as day consciousness kicked in, the battle started again.

During the second night on BiPAP, I was more alert. The two consciousnesses still had their battle while I was concentrating on my breathing. I realised the BiPAP was set too slow for normal breathing. I tried to trigger more breaths, but could do that only for a few breaths before the machine took over again. The harder I was trying to control my breathing the less I could achieve it. Eventually I went to sleep again. On awakening, my whole breathing had slowed down. I realised that was the Cheyne-Stokes breathing pattern, which is typical for a dying person. It consists of a number of breaths starting very low but increasing in length and intensity, followed by a long gap before the pattern starts again. This has to do with the chemical breathing triggers: oxygen and carbon dioxide. Normally, if the oxygen level or the carbon dioxide levels in the blood cross a certain threshold, the next breath will be initiated. Because the body wants to get rid of the CO2, these breaths are deep. The oxygen trigger does not work, therefore, a gap occurs until the CO2 levels are too high and the next cycle will be initiated.

I found myself confronted with this breathing pattern. A healthy person would simply initiate the next breath and fill the gap with breaths. I tried it, but was not strong enough to trigger the next breath. I found myself wanting to breathe and not being able to. The breaths of the other half of the cycle were overwhelming and blew me away. The sats were, in all of this, 99 percent. Staff commented on my slow breathing, but because my 'sats were fine they could not see a problem. Meanwhile, I was stuck in a cycle of either having too much air blown in my lungs or nothing. I was pretty desperate to escape this situation. I thought I needed to be precise, so I spelled on the word board: "the respirator is in Cheyne-Stokes modus." This did not make sense to my carer. I tried it differently and tried to spell out: "there are gaps and too much air." That did not make sense either, given that my sats were good. They assumed I was trying to get rid of this breathing aid, as I had tried to do so the previous day. But I realised the BiPAP is set too slow for normal breathing. Like the night before. I got desperate and communication broke down. They told me what I was saying did not make any sense.

 I gave up with this carer and put my hope in the day carer. As soon as she arrived, I spelled the whole thing again: "Cheyne-Stokes modus, too slow with gaps, too much air, I can not trigger it." She wrote it down, although it did not make sense to her either, given my good sats. She told the nurse, but the nurse could not connect anything with the name 'Cheyne-Stokes' and could also not see anything wrong, given my good sats. I was desperate. I had been fighting all night, but nobody could see a problem.

Facing death*

When the consultant came the same afternoon, I started again, trying to tell him what was wrong. He recognised the Cheyne-Stokes breathing pattern and the fact that I could not trigger the machine due to the weakness of my diaphragm and muscles of the chest. Thankfully, he changed the settings of the machine. He programmed it to give me 15 breaths per minute, which the machine would do regardless of my ability to trigger it.

This made me more comfortable with the respirator. I no longer had the feeling of needing to fight for my own breathing pattern. The next night, I started to have periods of sleep and finally [did] not have [to fight] both night and day.

This is how far Ute got with the work on her book.

* * *

> *As she was admitted to hospital, the final battle for her life had begun and I called her daughter to come over from Germany as soon as possible. Franziska arrived on Boxing Day and as we were driving from the airport to the hospital the doctor tried to reach me on my mobile phone, to tell me that Ute was dying and that I should come in as soon as possible. I never heard my phone while fully concentrating on getting there as soon as possible.*

When we arrived, Ute had – to everyone's amazement – turned a corner. She was 'back' beaming at us when she saw Franziska and me coming in. She spelled two words on the word board "too early..." I knew what she wanted to say and completed the sentence for her "...to give up" and she gave us a huge smile. Later, when the eye-gaze equipment was brought into the hospital, she shared with one of her carers the following:

She wrote that when it looked like she was dying, she found herself somewhere, where she was offered perfect peace. It was lovely. She felt that none of the people she loved held her back from letting go – the only reason why she came back was the book. It was not finished yet. Then she proceeded to write this last chapter while battling through two bouts of pneumonia and experiencing what she described above.

Hospital*, coming home* and farewells*
[Some names have been changed to protect confidentiality]

From her hospital diary and last communications

Saturday, 3rd of January 2015* From a conversation between Ute and myself in hospital, (taken from photos of the screen showing her words.)

I could have crossed the threshold at Christmas, that was on offer for me… the book was the reason [for me to keep fighting to live]. Nothing else [held me back from letting go], although I love the people around me, the book was the important issue.

The Demon had a laugh, telling me [probably 'asking me'] if I want duly to go through all the struggle when I could have peace. I was considering it, but the book was holding me back. Yes, all the struggle and misery with the BiPAP, I was offered to [be] let off. But that is the temptation.

I was fighting it for three days until I got through. [the worst of the first bout of pneumonia] Louise (not real name) told me when my sat's dropped everybody was running and the BiPAP was put on full speed. I wanted to pull the mask

[BiPAP] off. They tried to call you but you went to collect Franziska. I realised it needed a team and some cruelty to keep me alive. Thank God I had stated I want full treatment. [!] Was that Boxing day? Anyway I would go [would have gone, meaning would have died]

The BiPAP is the call for consciousness because it goes against normal breathing but you have to go through it fully consciously.

Tuesday 6th January 2015

(communication to her care staff)*

Nights

I feel unsafe with the BiPAP, because the mask creates a claustrophobic feeling. The respirator is so noisy that I often do not understand what is spoken to me. That slows my response down. To spell out on the word board, "I cannot hear, is too much effort. The other problem is the change of sides on the board [depending on how each individual carer held it up]. The letters might not be where I expect them to be. Often, I am frightened, particularly [when] coughing, because it brings phlegm only halfway up - enough to obstruct the airways, but not high enough to reach them with suction. One night, [I] needed clapping [upwards beats on the back, gentle but strong enough to help things move up] [and carers to lean [me] forward, [using] careful suction quite far back in my mouth.

I try to avoid coughing by [asking to be positioned so I am] sitting upright [in bed], and [for help with] finding the right position for the head. Too much forward helps with coughing, but creates a wet mouth and a head drop. Too much back creates a dry mouth and increased coughing. The head can slip to the right or the left. Therefore, I have little pillows in place. To find the right position with all this takes a while…if I have to cough, it takes even longer because of the frightening experience and the amount of suction I need.

The respirator creates either a dry and cold mouth or a wet and damp mouth. Particularly with the nebuliser, my mouth, face, and nose can be dripping wet. To avoid that, I like the tube of the respirator not lying in the bed but on the shortest route out of the bed and resting on the bedrail to take the weight of the nebuliser off my nose and keep the nebuliser horizontal.

My only intention is to sleep, but with not being able to clear my throat on the one hand and not being able to swallow on the other hand, this is difficult to manage.

In addition to all that, I have loose stools. I never know whether I produce air, wet air, and/or bowel action. The bedpan does not work with this sort of bowel action. I decided to bite the bullet and go incontinent [accepting incontinent pads]. It is at least less stressful.

Thursday 8th January 2015*

Last night I considered [to be] a good night because of no coughing and [no] anxiety. I went to sleep before 'the blood pressure round'. But I woke up with anxiety and the feeling of not having enough oxygen. It turned out that the plan was to wean me off the oxygen [after recovery from pneumonia]. That explained the low sats on the respirator and my levels of anxiety the [previous] two nights. The nurse turned the oxygen up to eight litres [last night]. That took the anxiety away. I went to sleep but woke up soon. The mask had slipped up, because the straps at the back of my head had slipped. The other issue was positioning; I [had] requested to be moved forward and back again because of friction at my back. I was moved with the headrest, which caused even more friction, resulting in pain in my left shoulder and left-upper back. The pressure areas were red in the morning. But with a change of position, it eased.

Wednesday, 14th January 2015 [diary]*

Third day of second diagnosed lung infection this time right lung. Not sure whether it has peaked already. Three days of constant use of BiPAP because I was too weak to breathe myself. Sats between 90 and 100. Last night was the first night of good sleep. I managed to keep a breathing rhythm with the machine by waiting until the machine initiates breath and concentrating on breathing out. That is how it works in sleep. When I am awake, I trigger the breath and the

Hospital*, coming home* and farewells*

BiPAP fills the gap. That is exhausting for me and produced Sats about 90 to 95.

Saturday, 17th January 2015 [diary]*

Had a reasonable night with Lorazepam[44], for evening personal care. Was dirty and frightened. Went to sleep straight away. On waking up Alice [a carer] was playing a sounding bowl, telling me Zambodhi had left[45]. I heard outside the night [staff] having a discussion, Zambodhi going home did not make sense, reality slipped. I tried to concentrate on the music but had colour impressions and another layer of information connected with the music. It was telling of new buildings with roof structures of lead and other things. I got confused and lost, what is reality here? Side effects of Lorazepam?

I managed some sleep but could not clear my throat. Alice used the suction machine [earlier] but did not get any of the thick stuff at the back of my throat, so I had to cope. For a moment I was close to panic; Alice had fallen asleep, I had no voice, so I had to cope.

Yesterday [16th January 2015] diary*

I had to fight anxiety. With morning care my sats dropped under 70% with a respirator. I felt the blood in my ears, the

---

44   Medication in this particular situation used to help with anxiety
45   I used to go and play sounding bowl music for Ute at the end of my working day. When I thought she had fallen asleep I went home, often after 1 am or even later in the early morning hours. However, many times she was probably not asleep but I needed to make sure I had some sleep myself.

obs[46] went up and I felt I had no air to breathe. This frightened me so much that I could not cope without the mask. I tried without it, but the blood pressure and respiration rate went up. So I went back on the BiPAP. Then I needed changing, this time with Lorazepam. That was no problem because my body felt strong as usual. And not shaky and weak.

24/25 January 2015*, [after her discharge from hospital, Ute's note to the night carers:]

The computer above my bed is not useful [any more]. I want it removed. I prefer the word board. My time is up and I need peace. Suction, mouth care, bed pan and moving me up in the bed – these are my basic needs. And when I need something different every minute, that is caused by the overwhelming fear that suddenly floods me, and not because I want to chase you around.

I try my best and I know you do too and I fail beautifully in the frightening moments. Thank you for your listening. You have seen how I have been fighting death in hospital. But now the time has come for me to surrender and let go. No, no tears, you are wonderful.

Thank you.

---

46   Heart rate, blood pressure and respiration rate

Hospital*, coming home* and farewells*

> *Ute's farewell to our father took place on the phone a few days before she died. She could hear him on the speaker and wrote her reply with the eye-gaze equipment in English, which Zambodhi translated for their father. Her last sentences were:*
>
> *"My body is packing in. My mind is clear. I have no more control over my life but trust that what is to come is good – as it always has been in my life."*

Part II

Memories and experiences with Ute
from carers, family, friends, and professionals.

Brief introduction to Part II by Zambodhi

As she stated in her introduction, it was Ute's wish that others would participate in the creation of this book, people who knew her and who had their own perspective on her situation, in order to create a **more balanced and objective picture**. It was left to me to follow this up after Ute's death and the interviews and written parts are presented in this part of the book. Perhaps Ute would have designed it differently and interwoven the perspectives of others in between her writings? There might have been more contributions but the time lapse since her death meant that I had lost contact with some key people during her illness. Instead I am pleased that five to eight years later there were still people ready to share their memories of Ute and their time with her and willing to contribute to this part of the book.

Lianne, one of Ute's main carers, doing all-day shifts

When I met Ute for the first time, I was thrown in at the deep end, so to speak. She was the first patient I was sent to see when I started working at the Care Agency and the first person I ever met diagnosed with MND. I received no explanations as to what I had to do; I was just quickly shown how to feed her and give her a cup of tea and then I was completely on my own.

I still remember when she asked to meditate and I prepared her for it. I told her to just call if she needed anything. More than an hour later, sitting in the carer's room in her home, I still hadn't heard a word from her and I looked in on her, a little worried. But that was a big mistake! She yelled at me for interrupting her.

That was difficult for me – I felt awful for interrupting her, and it was never fun to be yelled at. I really thought that I couldn't do this work and considered quitting.

But I went to my next shift with Ute anyway, and it was the best decision I've ever made. After this first experience,

Ute and I quickly developed a good relationship, which gradually turned into a friendship. Every morning I went to her and gave her breakfast. Then, a few months later, I turned on her computer and adjusted the camera, which read her eye movements. If everything was set up correctly, we could talk. My daughter, who was four at the time, adored Ute and asked me to visit Ute on my days off so that she could come with me. She wanted to go to the farm yard with me and Ute to look at the animals. That was a lot of fun for all of us.

There was a lot to laugh about while working with Ute. The best part was when she was outside in her wheelchair reading her newspaper one afternoon and the pigs had run away! Clare [Ute's friend and volunteer] and I had to run all around to try to get them back into the barn. While Ute watched the spectacle, she doubled up with laughter!

> *[When farmer Sam was given two pigs not as part of the farm flock but as his own, he needed to keep them somewhere safe. Sam thought it would amuse Ute, if she had pigs in line of sight at the bottom part of her long garden.]*

I am so grateful that I was able to meet Ute and take care of her. The fact that she trusted me to care for her and even entrusted me with showing others how to care for her meant a lot to me. She really was an inspiring woman. She showed great interest in me and other people and took in everything we said. She has had a huge impact on my life. When I'm confronted with difficult situations today and I can't imagine coping, I ask myself what Ute would say. And I know she's there to cheer me on and make sure I do the job to the best of my ability.

I feel privileged to have been there from the start when Ute needed 24-hour care, and also to have been there at the very end when she was able to end her life, so peacefully with the people she loved gathered around her bed. I think of her every day and make sure to talk about her with my children. I still remember the light in Ute's eyes when I told her I was pregnant with Olivia. She was so happy for me. Although Olivia never met Ute, she knows exactly who she is and what a great woman she was.

Ute taught me so much. She made me the caregiver I am today and I am forever grateful to her for that.

> *[Lianne and her partner now have a large family of seven children.]*

Christina, one of Ute's main carers, doing all-day shifts

I first met Ute in November 2013, when I became one of her main carers. I looked after her doing 12-hour shifts. At the time, I had no previous experience working with people diagnosed with MND. I will never forget when I met Ute for the first time. She was sitting by the window, enjoying the view and smiling when she saw me approaching.

As I spent four to five days per week with Ute, each time 12-hour shifts, I quickly learnt what Ute needed and wanted assistance with and we worked quite well together.

Ute wasn't able to swallow food and drinks without some considerable difficulties but this didn't mean she gave up on eating or drinking before she had to. Ute especially loved her large cup of tea, which was a real challenge to assist with, due to the high risk of her choking. I had to take up a specific position behind her wheelchair and while she could, she would still hold her hands on the cup. I assisted her with lifting the weight of the cup, guiding it to her mouth and tilting it just right so that not too much but enough tea would enter her mouth. This was the most difficult experience for me.

I became familiar with all of Ute's care needs quickly and I, and the rest of her team, had to adjust to the changes that her illness demanded. It became really hard when I or others in her team were paired up with an inexperienced carer. Ute became upset, especially when the new carers didn't listen to me or worse could not understand me. Ute's care needs were complex and people who didn't know her, could be scared of her screaming in desperation – but I knew that when she screamed, she was not just being difficult. There was always something wrong that urgently needed addressing. In the last month or two Ute struggled and got upset many times as she was unable to articulate what was wrong when moving and handling mistakes were made, most of which caused her discomfort or pain or put her at risk.

Ute used every free moment to finish her book on the computer, writing with the eye-gaze equipment. I learnt how to calibrate it for her and she had trained herself to write quite quickly with the movements of her eyes. Thereby she could 'say' what she needed quickly too.

Over time, we had to use the word board more often because calibrating the eye-gaze equipment for her in hospital was more complex. Communication became extremely challenging as Ute was fighting for her life in hospital and frequently we could no longer make sense of her attempts to spell words for us on the word board. It took a lot of concentration for Ute (and for us) and her strength was dwindling;

sometimes we didn't understand her needs and had to give up, which was heartbreaking. At that time my shift hours with Ute were much reduced by my manager, who realised that I was very close to Ute and knew how difficult it was for me to witness her suffering. Often I returned very upset from my shifts with her.

Throughout my time working with Ute I learnt a lot for myself. She changed my life completely. I will never forget the times when we laughed, our time spent on the farm and her advice on taking decisions in my life. She was the strongest woman I ever met and I will always be proud that I have had the privilege and pleasure to know her.

I have taken care of two more people with the same condition since, but nothing was the same. The magic of her spirit to fight for life was gone, and they just weren't Ute.....

Ute was a strong woman. Although she knew full well what her illness meant and that she would die of it, she was putting up a fight and not giving in at all. Ute will be forever in my heart and I will never forget her.

[Christina had another child after Ute died and is working and looking after her family together with her husband.]

Callie, one of Ute's main day time carers

I started working at the nursing agency in July 2014 and was still in my introduction period when I met Ute. In the beginning I only visited her in the mornings and evenings, as I did not yet have the training required for day care. At that time my duties included washing and dressing her in the morning and putting her to bed in the evening together, with another member of staff. That's how I slowly got to know Ute and her needs, to which I adapted my care approach. We grew closer, and I could feel her trust in me growing steadily.

It became a need for me to do what was best for Ute, and so I asked to be assigned to her on a regular basis and to be trained to cover all aspects of Ute's care. After completing the training in handling the feeding tube, I was able to work as part of Ute's daycare team.

Although this was associated with a lot of joy for me and Ute, there were also some challenges. Ute, however, didn't want us to struggle and helped us as much as she could. We often took her in her wheelchair around the farm yard, and once I was working with Ute when we took a taxi to a concert in the cathedral.

During some difficult times in my life I felt stressed, helpless and hoped that I wouldn't lose her respect because of it. To my surprise, Ute wasn't like that at all; she was patient and understanding and she wanted to make things easier for me and others, explaining everything as best she could. She also taught me how to prevent things and was friendly and very helpful. She was a role model for never taking life for granted and living it to the fullest. During the day care I was able to feed her, give her all the medicines and give her the famous cup of tea by the mouth, that I usually shared with her – but on my clothes. She really was like a ray of sunshine and always ready for a smile, regardless of her condition and suffering. Ute really made me feel valued.

To my delight, we remained good friends and very close until Ute finally took her last breath and continued on her way. It was such a joy to be with her all the time, including the moment of her death, and everything that was done came with love and devotion.

The fact that I was able to have this experience right at the start of my career made me the person I am today. I have so much more patience now, and it taught me never to take things for granted – there are always people who desperately need help. I had a wonderful experience with Ute and I can't imagine having an opportunity quite like this again. That's what makes it so special. She was one of a kind and a valued member of our team. My help to her was meaningful and it taught me how to help other patients who are in the same or similar situations. Ute's family made us feel special and she was always so grateful for the help she received.

She was really an inspiration to me! She met my kids and we had fun, spending a lot of time together. Ute had a big impact on my life and also on my heart. She was a role model for a young girl like me, who was still doing a lot of growing up.

[Callie is now working in a health centre and raising her three children.]

Marcus, a voice from the family

The following was written by our cousin, Marcus.

When the sisters visited us in Germany in the Summer of 2012, it felt like a farewell tour for Ute. She had metal splints for her feet and lower legs with her, with the help of which she could walk and climb stairs—with difficulty. Her disability was already so evident that the serious and mysterious illness she suffered from cast a deep shadow. Regardless, Ute was very bright and cheerful at our little family gathering.

In the months that followed, news kept coming about Ute's deteriorating state of health. For this reason I decided, in June 2013, to come to England and visit her in Stroud for a week. During this week, I had the opportunity to spend time with Ute almost every day. We had long and deep conversations, during which I was particularly impressed by her profound knowledge, e.g. about the history of the English Midlands, including Roman prehistory.

We spent some time at her favourite place, the farm, where we made a typical biodynamic preparation and sprayed it for plant growth. Ute was very enthusiastic when the water got to the desired consistency after stirring it, creating ever new vortexes for a long time! I then got to do the honourable task of spraying the result of the one-hour stirring onto the field. The next task was to harvest chamomile flowers. It was clear that her vision of it was far faster than I could complete the task!

Ute was in her element on the farm. I can still see her in front of me as she went across the uneven fields on her scooter, despite being hardly able to hold onto it any more.

Our trips to Gloucester and Oxford were nice. I also liked how easy it was to organise a scooter on site and also how it was possible for the three of us to visit everything we wanted to see. Gloucester Cathedral had a lift that Ute could use, sitting on the scooter to get to the level of the altar. Of course, she wanted to see it up close. She was so familiar with church history, too.

I did not see Ute again before she died, but I got to experience how she made her way through this stage of her illness. I fondly remember her ability to live the best she could, staying positive and having fun.

Interview with Denise, then manager of the care agency

Zambodhi: Hello Denise, and thank you for your willingness to attend this interview about your work with Ute. Please describe how you got to know Ute and became involved in working with her.

Denise: I was first introduced to Ute due to a complaint, which the district nurse had put in with regard to Ute's care. It was about what her carers were not doing right and what they were not doing at all when needed. I was new to the post of registered manager in that branch of the agency. I think it must have been my first or second day in the office and I responded with some urgency because obviously the district nurse had a good reason to put in a complaint. I went straight out there to visit Ute, to introduce myself and find out about the problems.

From the first moment, I worked very closely with Ute. She told me a bit about herself, from one health care professional to another and that made a huge difference in our relationship. It was not a client – manager relationship at all. We were on the same level as professionals and that made life very easy for me, as Ute actually had a lot more knowledge than I did in many areas. It was great that we could share professional experiences. Ute was able to pass on her information and knowledge and she loved doing that. She was a very good teacher – not only to me, but to the carers as well.

One of the main problems with Ute's care was that the care staff, who were doing their best, did not have the necessary training. A lot of them were not able to speak English well enough to understand all of the instructions and the culture here. That was a big hurdle because Ute's care was already quite complex and becoming more and more so. Ute and I worked out together what we needed to resolve urgently and where we needed a longer-term plan.

The first thing I did was identify the right people to work with Ute. The key people were still very young[47] but had already built a relationship of trust with Ute and were willing to learn and adjust as her needs changed. Together with Ute, we identified the carers she wanted to continue working with and with that began the building of her team. It became a diverse group of all walks of life, all age groups and was

---

47 [in their early twenties. All of the carers above are included in this group.]

Interview with Denise, then manager of the care agency

very international. Subsequently, a male carer, with whom Ute made a very good connection, became part of the team. I gathered that under previous management, carers were sent out on a daily basis, according to availability and time efficiency but not with respect to familiarity with clients and their specific needs. Even in complex cases they were assigned without regard to the skill set needed or language adequacy. The rotas were not well coordinated and there was a lot of work to do to change that during the following few months.

With Ute's team I made sure all members knew Ute well, as they had to learn and almost daily grow and develop with the changing of her care needs. Part of the team were also a few people who could step in, so that if anybody left or was unavailable they were equally well trained and did occasional shifts with Ute to keep themselves updated. Her team knew what she liked and disliked and would be able to recognise when she had a bad day or a good time. This was necessary in order to provide client-centred care. Once the team had been established, I started introducing the OT, the Physiotherapist and Speech and Language therapists and we had meetings and training with them for the team. And then I would go in independently and speak to Ute, making sure that everything was all right. She was good at giving me feedback. The interprofessional cooperation expanded and with that Ute's quality of life improved.

Through conversations with the agency staff, as I got to know them better, it emerged that the previous manager seemed to have kept quite well away from the situation around Ute's case, and I did not like that. She needed people with the right skills, people she could trust with this journey she was on. I needed to match her carers well, so it would work psychologically too.

I used to visit quite often, linking with other agencies involved in her care. Ute welcomed and requested this. For example she asked me to link with the physiotherapist and the occupational therapist, and subsequently I could ensure all carers had regular training updates from the physiotherapist to do daily passive limb movements, in order to keep the joints mobile and to prevent spasms and discomfort as much as possible. It worked as a team effort, including the meetings with Ute and four or five professionals at the time. I also noticed the carers need for support, which changed in accordance with the progression of Ute's illness. It was important to have very good communication in place, so updates and updated training were available. Equally important was psychological support, making adjustments and taking the carer's needs into consideration, especially in the last phase of Ute's illness.[48] While all staff were respecting confidentiality, Ute made her own decisions with regards to divulging more information and getting closer to some of her carers. She touched many hearts the way she met people.

---

48   As described above by Christina

Interview with Denise, then manager of the care agency

The work at her home took place in a warm atmosphere, consolidating and gathering around the ever-changing situation. Even the Motor Neuron Consultant for Gloucestershire and the MND coordinator were part of this and it worked beautifully. It's actually almost a model case of how things should be done, with everybody communicating. That, I think, gave Ute the quality of life she wanted to have – given the bad luck she was in, having this illness.

Zambodhi: On a more personal note: what did Ute bring into your life?

Denise: It is her knowledge of the world and that she was such a visionary. Very in touch with the land and for me in that there was like a whole package. It was easy for me to associate with Ute and to understand where she was coming from, what she wanted and how she felt. It was almost like not going there as a clinical professional, but something different, more like meeting a colleague, perhaps also because Ute was trained and still working as a nurse when we first met.

Ute brought the quality of our relationship into focus for me. It was possible to have such an honest relationship with her. The conversations frequently diversified from one thing to another. I learned an absolute treasure trove of information from Ute through her wide knowledge base. We shared knowledge as professionals. I felt that she trusted me – which was a big gift from someone facing increasing vulnerability and death in the end.

I felt that she wanted to embrace me, as myself, as who I was. That allowed for something like a window into her mind. I could work out with her what she needed, and in what way the agency and the carers practically could assist. We bounced things off with each other until we got to the resolution. Similarly when the level of assistance needed adjustment, we worked out together what it was and how to do that.

I believe because Ute had this kind of connection to people that created a rather profound human experience and I think you do connect in that way as well. Ute's interest in the stars and in working with the earth may seem quite crass but it's not. It is something that I associate with and I believe in as well. We are all connected in some way. Nature, nurture – it is so important and it gets lost in everyday business of life. But it wasn't lost in Ute's home. You could have conversations about books, art, work, the stars and the heavens, trees, fields and animals. That was all part of Ute's care in many ways. And it became part of mine and Ute's shared world.

I find Ute's connectedness to every aspect of life quite pertinent and it helped me when sometimes it was quite strenuous for me. When I became quite anxious about the whole situation, this connectedness helped me to inwardly step back and understand. It also made it clearer in how I needed to speak with you and how I could help you as well as Ute. From the time I met Ute and her family and you – well I can feel it right to now and I suppose it had a profound effect on me. Something like this does not happen often.

Interview with Denise, then manager of the care agency

Zambodhi: It sounds like meeting Ute has still an effect on your life now – is that so?

Denise: Yes, it is. It is interesting to realise the impact that some people and some things can have on you as a person and I am pleased that I have been able to recognise that. I think some people maybe would not notice when it happens to them. Maybe it is because I'm older and a bit wiser, it was a very emotive period of time. And it was good.

Zambodhi: Thank you for sharing this, Denise. Hearing your perspective, especially when when the stress levels were high, makes me appreciate even more what you did. I can still feel the appreciation for your holistic approach to caring for Ute. What mattered to Ute became your focus, and you with Ute's team went so much beyond the expected tasks of caring. It was special, that the carers wanted to learn about the PEG feeding, moving and handling, the suction machine, the physio and that they were willing to accompany Ute on special occasions to a concert or an exhibition, moving their care shift to much later in the night, to help Ute into bed. All with full back-up from you. How we worked even closer together, as things became more complex with the same human focus at the core, fills me with gratitude to this day.

Denise: Yes and the trouble we got in, when Ute went into hospital, do you remember? The carers went into A & E with her on Christmas Eve with my full backing, staying and looking after her as they had done in her home. And it was the right thing to do!

> *[The carers by her bed assisted with moving and handling and communication and meeting Ute's needs as described above. Hospital staff trained the carers with use of BiPAPP and nasal oxygen as well as suction. This inevitably brought competency conflicts and was a difficult field to negotiate for everyone].*

Zambodhi: Yes, they had to call the medical staff for assistance several times in the first 24 hours. Ute was unable to alert anyone and if they had not been with her she would have died then. When I realised how serious her situation was, I also knew that Ute needed her carers. She would have had no chance to survive without being able to communicate and without the people who knew her well there observing changes and alerting hospital staff. I felt for the other patients with the same illness in hospital without such close personal support. I hope this will change at some point soon. Hospital staff do not have the time to sit with people and learn their communication systems.

Denise: Yes, and I had a lot of grief and many phone calls trying to get funding for this level of care in the hospital. People that sit in their offices look at things differently, of course. Only thanks to the Christmas holidays did we get a week or so of funding, then it was cancelled as you know.

Interview with Denise, then manager of the care agency

> *[Denise should have pulled out of providing care when Ute was admitted to hospital. Instead she agreed with the family's view, that Ute would be completely helpless and unable to communicate at all without her skilled carers' support. She argued for further funding of a highly complex care package when the offices opened again but it was turned down, which we expected.]*

Now we can look back at having done it nevertheless, it's happened and we are all happy with it.

Zambodhi: This was one of the best things we could do for Ute staying with her in hospital. With breathing difficulties anxiety can be a big struggle. While Ute was in the respiratory ward, there was one other person on the ward with the same condition, without anybody by their bedside 24/7. Knowing that Ute could not have made any sound louder than the machines surrounding her bed and that the BiPAP mask dislodged so many times, creating discomfort and not working properly as a result, I shudder to think how the other patient was experiencing their situation. Ute's need for suctioning, moisturising her lips and mouth, readjusting the mask and dealing with other discomforts frequently, could not have been met without someone by her bedside all of the time observing her and knowing her well. In a busy hospital staff do not have much time to spend with patients let alone to learn the communication systems.

At this late stage in her life, Ute's situation created a new model of care, a combination of hospital and community care. And you did allow it to be tried out by agreeing to support it. You could have said that the hospital is 24/7 care and therefore the agency would have to withdraw from Ute's care altogether. Most likely she would have remained unable to communicate and not been able to come home to die. But instead you supported Ute's carers in adjusting to their new role in hospital. They did their best to show hospital staff how to move Ute and they enabled her to communicate with the eye-gaze equipment and the word board and they were trained by the hospital staff supported by your agency in how to deal safely with nasal oxygen, the BiPAP mask etc. It was tough on everybody. But as a result Ute could be discharged home when the time came for her to let go.

Denise: I think that she would have deteriorated quite rapidly in hospital, if the carers hadn't been constantly there, because the nurses didn't have time to check on her that often.

Interview with Denise, then manager of the care agency

Zambodhi: It is most likely that Ute would have died very quickly after her admission. Recalling the reports I got from the carers, which stated that in the first 24 – 48 hours they had to go repeatedly and alert medical staff to attend to Ute quickly (because of the drastic decrease of oxygen levels) was saving her life at that stage. I know doctors expected Ute to die on Boxing day, when I fetched Franziska[49] from the airport.

Denise: They reported this to me as well.

Zambodhi: So here we have a precedence of care if you like, because in the traditional view, hospital care equals 24/7 care. In practice, as evident with the complexity of Ute's needs, it doesn't.

What influence does knowing Ute have on your life now?

Denise: I don't do tick boxes, I think that is what Ute inspired me to do. Care is about the client. I learned from Ute how critical it is to work closely with the client, particularly in complex cases. When I get a care package from Social Care they are all the same, like thirty minutes in the morning, washing, dressing, breakfast etc. When I take on a new client now, I look at what matters to the person, what makes them enjoy their lives. For one it may be the shiny furniture, for another it is something else. In one case we have taken on the care of a dog that has been with the client for a long time and

---

49   Her daughter

now the client is unable to care for it, but it matters so much that it is there.

Zambodhi: Thank you for your time and your sharing, Denise.

> *[Denise moved on to run her own care agency where she continues to develop her approach of client-centred care. Together with her clients and teams, she shapes care packages around each person's individual needs.]*

Interview with Margaret, General Manager at Horsfall House Care and Nursing Home

Zambodhi: Thank you for agreeing to be part of this conversation, which takes place almost five years after Ute's death. As you know, Ute worked on her book in the last months of her life and she hoped that other people would be willing to contribute their perspectives to it, That takes me here to ask you about your experience in your role as manager of the nursing home and as Ute's supervisor: what was it like working with Ute, how did it change when Ute got ill and how do you see it now, looking back?

Margaret: I knew Ute as a nurse in the dementia unit, a capable, competent and kind nurse with a good understanding of this group of people. It is mainly older people, but also some younger adults with dementia in this department, with all the effects that the condition can have on how people function – for example, speaking, understanding and taking care of yourself.

Ute was a reliable employee. The nurse on duty is responsible for the shift. It is their responsibility to lead the nursing-assistant team and the nursing assistants will liaise with the nurse if they need to report anything or if anything else is going on. As a colleague, Ute was able to handle all these tasks professionally. She was straightforward, honest, intelligent and also logical in her thought processes. And those traits, both on a professional and personal level, were part of who she was. I think that helped her in her work here, and I felt that all of these qualities helped her when faced with a change in her own health situation. She was respected by our team, she was respected by another team as well as the visiting doctors, psychologists and social workers. They knew that in Ute they were dealing with someone who was a good advocate for the people she was responsible for.

When Ute began to feel unwell and finally reported on her diagnosis, she explained that prior to the diagnosis, she had been alarmed by her symptoms for some time, as is often the case with neurological disorders. The person experiencing the changes already has an idea that something is not quite right. So, getting the definitive diagnosis is the end of the story rather than the beginning. I still remember exactly how Ute told me about it. It was obvious that she wanted to do her absolute best and keep going, whatever her current abilities were, as long as time and ability would allow her to do so.

Interview with Margaret, General Manager at Horsfall House Care and Nursing Home

And here we also try to support people when they are going through changes in their life, so that what is best for them can be what is best, while of course we have to deal with the larger context. On this basis we sat down with Ute. With her approval, I included the support of our occupational health consultant in the process, to explore things that we might need to change in the workplace over time to help her to continue to function.

We could do that. And it was clear that we could and had to rely on Ute's honesty about her physical changes, because obviously there were some clear safety risks there, both for herself and for the people who are also vulnerable, i.e. the residents here. And also for her colleagues. So we entered into this cooperation very openly with one another. Ute knew that we would respect her as an individual, that we would respect her privacy and that we would respect her dignity. But there were also some professional responsibilities that she and we agreed to. So the deal was that we would be open and honest with each other without being nosy, and that she would be honest and open with us as soon as she noticed a change in terms of physical fitness, energy levels, or concentration levels. When it became apparent that her physical mobility issues had become problematic for her nursing work and could lead to difficulties and dangers for her, we were then able to discuss how we could utilise her nursing expertise in other ways.

And that led to Ute's participation in a project: updating all of our clinical and operational guidelines. This is a bit like the Forth Bridge. Once you finish updating it, you can start working on it all over again at the beginning. It was an advantage to have someone who had the knowledge, skills and time to help us with these things. That was Ute's new role. She was still employed here, still in her role as a nurse, but with a different administrative job. The number of hours she worked varied over time based on her own health needs and energy levels. But it meant for me that where I had a reliable resource, I could continue to use that reliable resource, and from Ute's point of view, she still felt valued and she added to the same bigger picture. This then continued to have a positive impact on the people using Horsfall House's services.

We made it possible for Ute to continue her work even when she was no longer able to be at Horsfall House and it became easier for her to work from home. So she had a virtual office at home. I remember visiting Ute at home, both in terms of my pastoral role, managing health and well-being at work, and in terms of my role as Ute's manager, to discuss her work and its results. It was a great privilege to be able to do that. There was always negotiation with Ute, but she still felt like a close team member – just a bit further away geographically, but not in terms of the quality of the bond.

I think the work she has done has been of great value. We acknowledged it as such when we had our department-head meetings. This reminds me now that Ute also attended one or two of these meetings to keep us updated on her activities. The heads of department meetings are a mix of care, day-care and residential-care managers, so Ute was able to sit down with them as well, get feedback and make sure the guidelines were being respected and implemented accordingly.

Zambodhi: Was Ute the first employee with a life-threatening diagnosis for whom you were responsible as supervisor?

Margaret: I have had experience of this in the past, but this was the first time I had been asked for help at work by someone with this neurological condition. The condition is not unknown to us however, because some residents here live with MND too. So it was neither new territory nor an everyday situation, but not beyond probability and possibility. As I said before, an integral part of my expectation is to help people, as an employer that values people who are going through a difficult time in whatever circumstances, even if it is life-limiting. If we can secure a safe continuation of working hours at the employee's request, we will try to do so.

The Horsfall House Board of Directors helped me and Ute go through the process. They are the leadership team above me – I am the General Manager – and they understood that I would update them on how things were going. They realised that this was a staff member who still had something to give, although due to physical limitations she would give it in a different way.

Zambodhi: For Ute it was like a lifeline. At no time was she told that this was 'The End', that she could no longer be useful. At one point she said, "Now I think I will have to resign from my job at Horsfall House." But it was on her own terms.

Margaret: Yes, and that's exactly what she did. That's right, Ute was in control, she made the decisions when the moment was right for her. We had regular exchanges about it, but it was Ute whose decision making set the time frame. And it was good for her, I think.

Zambodhi: This experience of Ute's gave me a new perspective – a perspective on what is possible and how creative solutions can develop step by step.

I remember when Ute was no longer safe to walk, and you and the unit manager had a conversation with her. She came home that day and announced, "I was dismissed today." Then she grinned and continued, "And I've got a new job!" The new job was the administrative nursing post you had created for her. She knew she was still wanted at work and would have full support. It enabled her to do what she could still do and thereby add meaning in this stage of her life.

Margaret: Yes, and it was evident that she still had things she wanted to do despite realising that her time was limited.

Interview with Margaret, General Manager at Horsfall House Care and Nursing Home

Zambodhi: And that was sometimes possible and sometimes not so easy. Also, the gift to Ute was that you, Margaret, were not afraid of the struggles she had with the knowledge of what was happening to her.

I remember how difficult it was for her to share the news in the workplace just after her diagnosis. I kept asking Ute if she had said anything at Horsfall House. She replied, "No, I have to find the right moment." But the moment was never right... When I asked her if she made an appointment to discuss the issue, she sighed and asked to be left alone. It was a battlefield for her and she had to fight her way through[50] You helped her with that first interview, and I remember the impact your letter had on Ute after the conversation where Ute finally shared her news. It was very objective and summarised the new information you had received and outlined how you both wanted to work together from that point forward based on trust and sharing open and honest information. At the same time it was warm and full of empathy. Ute gave me your letter to read, it made her confident that there would be a good way for her to continue working.

Margaret: Of course, formal correspondence must be in place, as this is good practice and also provides a good basis for reflection upon which further discussion can be built. The written word is often a good reference point, isn't it?

---

50   This is different in my memory from how Ute remembers it. It is not important who is correct but that everyone's contribution creates a fuller picture.

Zambodhi: Yes, and the letters to Ute were so positive. Just as you appreciated Ute's work, she was able to relax, in that regard, at a time when she was dealing with many scary things. And that helped a lot.

I hope other employers in similar situations will feel encouraged to work with their employees should they wish to keep working and to contribute to a greater whole.

Margaret: That would be a good result!

Excerpt from the response to Ute's resignation from her work as a nurse at Horsfall House

Dear Ute,

....

This brings me back to your resignation letter of March 31, 2014 and your email today in response to my email of April 3, 2014 asking you if you really wanted to stop working for the company. Since you have confirmed that it is definitely your choice, there is nothing the company can do but accept this termination...

I would like to take this opportunity to thank you, dear Ute, for your work at Horsfall House over the last seven years, both in practical nursing and more recently, administratively. The work you have done on policies, procedures and related care documentation is exemplary. Your colleagues will miss you and want me to pass on their best regards to you. Like me, they found your tolerance and adaptability to the disease inspiring. You have dealt with so many personal and physical changes without complaint.

We wish you peace and serenity with your family and dear friends for the coming months.

Please let me know if there's anything else I can help you with.

Kind regards,

Margaret ...., Manager

Farmer Mark

Ute first came to work with us at the farm at Hawkwood in 2007, not too long after she had moved to the UK. My first impression was of a very strong, hard working, friendly person who was quite a strident and passionate farmer. She volunteered a few hours here and there at first but we got on well and soon employed her part time. She was also nursing part time, another very physical job.

Ute could be given to catastrophising at times, if a cow seemed poorly, she would warn us of the worst outcome, if a crop didn't seem okay, she would recall an experience when she had seen a whole crop die. Invariably these catastrophes never materialised. So, when she first noticed a foot drop and unstable walking, she told us the "worst-case scenario", which would be MND, and I thought, "Yeh yeh, that's Ute being Ute". This compounded the shock and horror I felt when she actually was diagnosed with MND. I knew enough about it to know that this was indeed "the worst-case scenario".

And so we entered a period of Ute gradually losing her strength, coordination, and physical abilities. This progressed from occasionally stumbling, to regularly stumbling, to falling down, falling down and needing help to get back up, needing assistance for many tasks, till it became too taxing to work on the farm at all. Yet, through all of this Ute had a profound positivity. I remember a day when we went out to the field to hand weed a crop of cabbages. Ute crawled along the row on her hands and knees pulling weeds from the ground. When she got to the end of the row I was instructed to get behind her, grab hold of her trousers on each side of her hips and haul her to her feet. Then she could stretch and, with muddy knees and grubby hands, get down to begin the next row. She could work as hard and efficiently as I could but couldn't get up without my assistance. There were many jobs on the farm that she could do with the right help and organisation but as time went on these slowly became too wearing and tiring for both Ute and us, the farm team and eventually, in 2013 the time came to end her employment on the farm. Although I enjoyed working with Ute and she was pulling her weight, I have to say it was a relief when she decided to quit.

We had a discussion during one lunch break when I had the gall to ask her thoughts on assisted suicide. She completely engaged with the discussion and clearly said something along the lines of, "I will do everything necessary to live my life to the fullest until I die". And that is exactly what she did. With the help and love of Zambodhi (who supported her throughout her illness) and her friends she made the most of her life within the strictures of this very serious disease.

I occasionally spent time with Ute when she had deteriorated to the stage of needing full-time care, not being able to walk, talk, or feed herself. She was living in a bungalow on the farm and I would eat my lunch with her. Conversation via the eye-recognition computer was painfully slow and it could be hard work to be there, but her humour and positivity still showed through. There were times when she felt so bad, physically, that I was refused an invitation to come in. Nothing about that time was easy, and when the bad times outweighed the better times, Ute announced that she had decided to let go and allow herself to die.

We hold a ceremony each February 2nd on the farm, Candlemas or Imbolc, a ceremony that was special to Ute. We make candles and light them in various places on the farm to welcome in the beginnings of spring. When Ute was in her last days at the end of January 2015, along with the farm candles we made one for her. I took the candle to her on the 2nd of February. Because of the danger with the oxygen cylinders in her bedroom, I could not bring it to her bedside. Ute was not conscious at the time but there were people keeping vigil. She died later that day, with the candle still going, held up by the tree outside her bedroom window where I put it so she could see it if she woke up. I don't think I will ever know anyone else who can face their mortality and degeneration with such dignity and strength.

Farmer Sam

I worked on the farm with Ute for two years before she was diagnosed with MND. She then continued to work, albeit less and less, for another two years. Ute understood how farmers relate to learning their craft. Some of the time it needs to go through experience rather than learning it by the books. She accepted our occasional rejection of her insights and observed us having the experience of the consequences without judgement. She was such an intrinsic part of the farm. During the second year of my working here her foot started catching. That was exactly the same as my mum had, when her MS developed. Stumbling and falling increased over time. For a long time Ute's arms remained strong, which enabled her to compensate a lot. I can still picture her pushing a wheelbarrow up one of the fields here and her knee knocking against the other one, somehow the knee would always keep giving in sideways. She would plod along wearing her knee braces and other equipment. It was so good that she was up to a very practical approach to dealing with her disease because sympathy was not available in spades here. I think it is because farm people deal with life, death and illness every day. If we were overly sentimental it would be impossible to do the work. The farm is part of the cycle of life.

I thought about what I could do to enable her to carry on working, which is what she wanted. This focus also helped me to cope with what happened to Ute in front of everyone's eyes. So there may also be an element of keeping down emotions about it. I valued Ute's knowledge, experience and skills on the farm. Supporting her best we could was no charity. It was great to work with her for as long as possible. She had given so much to the farm over the years and it felt like we owed it to her – it was the least we could do.

Luckily Ute had a great sense of humour. When she fell over with the backpack sprayer she just lay there like a tortoise on her back. Before I picked her up, we had a good laugh about how silly it looked, then we just got on with the work. Laughing at times is so good – it is probably a combination of a coping mechanism and a relief too.

Ute moved into our family home for about two months (as a transitory solution) when she was unable to get up the stairs to the flat. This was in the summer, when my wife and children stayed with her family for a month or so. Ute and I got on fine and when everyone was back, it was nice to have Ute as an addition to our family. I believe it was a real gift for our girls too. They were used to elderly people with disabilities in my mother-in-law's home and they knew Ute quite well. We shared similar values, having our meals together and family and farm chats during those times.

I was amazed by the occupational therapist, how quickly all the aid was organised and installed, like the ramp across the lawn outside our front door, grab handles everywhere, and when she saw that something was needed and within a few days she would bring it. However, when Ute's deterioration reached the stage that she needed personal care, our family home could no longer accommodate her needs. Everything needed more time and space, a hoist and other equipment was needed. She left us when Social Services found an interim solution. I was pleased when she eventually became our neighbour, moving into the bungalow next door, with carers being in there day and night.

The spirit over the physical comes to mind when thinking of Ute, it was the spirit she had and a mindset so much stronger than her body, which was falling apart. Ute kept her work up as far as she possibly could have done.

However, there were tough moments too. I remember she said that she hoped that something almost telepathic would develop when speech would fail her. The hardest for me was later in her illness, when she clearly wanted to tell me something but could not get it across.

I think that leads to where I am today. There was a profound change when Ute could no longer work with us. She had a balancing influence on the farm. Not that we did not do a good job, she just was such a steady, rational influence, contributing with her in-depth knowledge and pragmatic approach. Ute has had both a life-changing and life-affirming influence on me just because of who she was and being around her. She has changed my views on and awareness of disability – access, people's ability to do things, even when it looks initially impossible to me.

It was Ute's unwavering belief in the power of trust that stayed with me. That was quite something to have in her situation, including trust that the right thing will happen and how important it is to be open to it. I think that is where I am right now. How could I leave the farm otherwise with the inner knowledge that it is time for me to move on but with nothing else lined up? I learnt so much about trust from Ute, and now I trust that the right thing will come along.

When I was in that decision-making process I sat here at the farm on Ute's memorial bench and had a real distinct feeling – it was almost as if I could hear a voice saying 'You need to make a decision, you cannot muddle along like this. Either commit or leave.' That was a wake-up call, having this clearly put in front of me. I had been asking myself, *what would Ute say?* This wasn't telling me what to do, just clarifying that the current situation was not working well for me. My mind split between two places. 'Give this everything or move on from it', was so helpful. It was quite stark, really. And that is exactly what she would have said. Looking back at this moment, it is easy to see, she said the obvious at a time when it was not obvious to me. She had no fear of taking a step into the unknown. If you really openly enter into it and trust something will work out, it *will* work out. I have seen that working for Ute so many times, and now, following in her footsteps, it has begun working for me.

I believe Ute gave her life to her work – I never saw her in her other profession but I can only imagine that she was as committed and gave everything to nursing as well. She was still teaching her carers when she was receiving care. But is it not wonderful that at the same time she had no qualms about pulling anyone up when they were not doing things right, pointing it out and instructing them in the correct way of doing it? We appreciated it on the farm and her carers loved her for it. There are other people who could tell them how to do their job and that might have resulted in some resistance at times but when Ute did so, they accepted and became better at their jobs because of it. She had that way of communicating that did not upset people because it was so open and honest and matter of fact. I think it was that her comments and advice did not come with any judgement. And that made all the difference.

Apprentice Vasilios

We came to the farm in April 2013, and I was working with Ute until shortly before she died.

I believe it was not by chance that we met and I could relate to Ute differently. Interestingly she died on my mother's birthday. How we experience someone else's journey is actually a reflection of our own life experience. I could see how Ute's journey brought up experiences with my mother. My mother didn't have the same condition as Ute, she had cancer. She was ill for a long time, and I was her carer. My mother was a fighter as well, living beyond her predicted life expectancy.

When we go through our own journey, we either fill in any gaps that were left behind or we just pave the way for experiences to come. Perhaps my experiences with my mother paved the way for what was to come with Ute?

When I came to the farm I decided to stay in one place to learn there, as opposed to travelling around other farms, working on each one for a while. I was interested in more in-depth learning and found I could do that here.

It was a longer process to get used to Ute's style of teaching and not easy at all in the beginning because she had perhaps too much will. She used to say, "Well, these kinds of people (that I had encountered in my journey with biodynamic agriculture) don't know a thing and here we do things differently." I had to cover the learning units for two years in just one year. Strictly speaking, I did not have to do it, but Ute drove it at this rate! When it became harder for her to speak and move, I studied the material we could not cover on my own. But I could see more than that, I could see that behind all of this she had this drive to get through as much as possible, as quickly as possible. She had lots of experience with biodynamic farming, especially with the animals. She could see problems develop before anyone else could, but she also had the wisdom to let others learn by their own experience.

In the last few months of her life, things changed and that led to another level of connection. The learning units became secondary. We discussed life and Anthroposophy[51]. I had met Anthroposophy and the whole anthroposophical movement, coming from quite a different and diverse spiritual background. We reached a different level of understanding. The most important thing was the kind of sharing between us and also her openness to my experiences. With the awareness

---

51   Anthroposophy (from Greek Anthropos - the human being and Sophia - wisdom) - founded by Dr Rudolf Steiner in 1912, an Austrian philosopher, scientist and artist, who postulated the existence of a spiritual world comprehensible to pure thought and fully accessible only to the faculties of knowledge latent in all humans.

of the past, acknowledging the present we talked about working for the future. That became our new work together and we were doing it without anyone knowing.

Looking back now, I can see the transformation of the will, which is really important. The person I met at the beginning was full of sheer will, with a drive to do things and the knowledge of how it should be done. Ute had this relationship to her life, having taken on duties and obligations with her work and she had the wish to develop a local community, which is the concept of the community-supported farm, the CSA[52] model of farming. And this CSA practised the biodynamic method, a way of farming that Ute was deeply committed to, and that in turn was the root to her involvement in teaching apprentices. These were the things she was asking and striving for.

Later on in her illness, the whole thing transcended into something different, with no pressure and no striving. It was just happening and everything was falling into place. That was beautiful to experience; the community was there. She has such an influence on all of us.

The transformation of the will is something that has to do with the "I" – the higher self. She would agree with me that the greatest lesson is the transformation of the will into the real will, the higher will. Laughter and acceptance brings

---

52   CSA (Community Supported Agriculture) Community based farm co-operative, in this case, based on biodynamic farming principles. https://stroudcommunityagriculture.org/about-sca/,
https://dynamics.folio3.com/blog/biodynamic-farming/#what-is-biodynamic-farming

a different kind of understanding and connection to that part of the self, the I. This transformation stands out when I look back, and it is something I will never ever forget. How peacefully she was in herself, just lying there when she was not able to talk. There were moments, of course, when a lot of tension was in the air when we tried to give her her homoeopathic medication and things didn't work out, but then again there were these other moments, with this peaceful presence of hers, in fact the whole room felt like that and those were the most precious moments. Time either ceased to exist or seemed to expand somehow.

I can see the influence of Ute's journey on more people than just on myself. The people that were around her, such as her carers and everyone else involved in activities with or caring for her. Many arrived at the scene with conventional thinking and understanding of life. They were exposed to what went on in Ute's home, they looked after her needs all day and they experienced these practical study groups, such as the conscious nutrition group, the star group and the meditation group – and the carers were present during some of it. There have been eye openers for people from a completely different background. There were so many moments in her home that could not be experienced anywhere else and that was part of the journey we all experienced.

Reflecting now, I realise I miss Ute – I miss those moments. After she died I kept a connection with her and followed her progress. And later on I felt when Valerie [a close friend and neighbour] died and she joined her there.

I felt that Ute was fine and making progress where she is. It is important for us to make a connection when people have died, and we accompany that consciously. That is also the process of our own healing if we do such a thing.

Maria

My husband and I met Ute when she was still mobile in April 2013. We were living on the farm, and Ute and I had a lovely soul connection right from the beginning, one with clarity and honesty at the core. Looking back, it feels like a big honour to have walked that path with her. When we met Ute, she was physically able to do most tasks but soon I could see the transition slowly happening – the progression of her illness.

Ute and I had many conversations and deep sharing over morning and afternoon teas. Ute had to slow down from her physical activities and it was a period of big change in my life too. While her body was deteriorating (the person), the soul was present, and this is who I felt I knew throughout our time together. Even when the physical difficulties advanced, I never lost that connection with her; in fact it grew, and I was confident she did not lose it with me either.

Priorities felt different, being there with someone you love and seeing the restrictions unfolding in that person. At times I would feel a knot in my stomach seeing the challenges she had to face but I would take a moment to collect my feelings and let go because I wanted to be with her as a person and honour her for that.

Later she had to use a computer that voiced what she typed and verbal communication became slower. Then it was thinking about what else we could do with our time together, and at some point we chose a book to read. This book [*Initiation*, by Elisabeth Haich] took us on a big journey. Sometimes the reading felt astonishingly scary, because of the relevance to Ute's situation. At moments I needed to gather all my courage to carry on reading. And I could see it in Ute's eyes, when I looked at her, how intense and wide they were. It was certainly not light reading, but it brought us very close together. This also revealed to me the advancement and strength of her soul. She was not born yesterday…

In the later stages of her illness I had moments of feeling extremely sad, finding Ute's journey overwhelming. But then there were the other moments when I saw Ute's spirit, that she was shining through her illness. It seems strange to say that, but she was literally shining through all of it. I made a conscious choice to be with her on this part while acknowledging the parts of her life that were vanishing. The further the illness developed, the harder it became for her to express herself and there were times when emotions just had to come out, unfiltered. This was not always in accordance with how behavioural convention would expect it, but Ute was in this extraordinary situation and had huge restrictions in expressing her frustrations. During the reading I believe she had fearful moments[53] where it related so much to her own journey but there were many other moments when she was so radiant. She was so present.

One of the joyful memories that comes up for me are these two black pigs which Sam put in the bottom of her garden. And there were his chickens too. It was quite funny to observe them from Ute's living room, and they seemed to like the attention, coming up to the boundary to the middle and upper garden. The hens were hanging around and the pigs got their surprises with that. I could tell how much that made Ute at home, how much she enjoyed observing the interactions between the animals. Her observational skills were always advanced, and that didn't change.

Ute did not lose her personality or character in any way, and that was probably good for others too. When someone is changing, or there is such a huge amount of change on so many levels as was with Ute, confusion can arise for all. But she was still as organised as before; she kept an eye on things that needed doing around her care, even reminding others what needed doing at times. Whoever visited Ute, that person would have to give her homoeopathic medicine. It was complex, and all the drops, powders and pillules needed to be given correctly in a spoon the right way. But it wasn't just this. Ute was very particular, closely checking how many drops or pillules landed in the spoon so you felt the pressure more, and the fact that she had difficulties swallowing was

---

53 The book describes the journey of an Egyptian Initiate, at one point relating the experience of consciousness trapped in a mummified body.

the biggest challenge as we all feared she might choke. And sometimes she did. This task would include some moments of terror especially for those who did not have the confidence for the task. But by maintaining her personality, her beliefs, and wishes, Ute created stability for those around her.

I believe that keeping an eye on the details like this kept her going. And her knowledge on the practical level. She wanted everything so specific. The care team (and all of us) shouldn't loosen up too much!

What remains ingrained in my mind is the polarity – the contrast in her life. On the one hand, that human intensity of terror – these deep emotions were always there – in both of us. On the other hand was her light, her radiance and because I am quite visual I need to say, the verticality of her light and spirit that was fully present. This was a timeless moment in space while acknowledging the whole human journey she was going through. I observed how the spirit engages with the human journey and wondered how it might be necessary that the spirit may have to pass through some testing times or deep emotions on a human level before letting go. I always thought this moment would stay with Ute to reflect on and felt how amazing she was with such tremendous courage. Someone might say she did not have a choice, but I think she did. She had many choices all along how to live under these circumstances.

And I always thought of her sister too, how courageous and brave she was walking that path with her. That was the other thing that stayed with me. Zambodhi had to put her life on hold to do this. It was a lot to take on and it showed her tremendous love and devotion to Ute.

What has been left with me is the spirit of connectedness, naked, stripped to the bone to our simple humanness. How the people that came together just poured their love forth, and we all connected. Something our society should encourage more in everyday life. The time and care each person shared with Ute and her situation created a meaningful community through love. This connection shows the magnificence of our being and the potential we have as individuals and society. I celebrate that. Everything else seems minor.

Later on when I went through the first years of Lyme disease my body was numb and so stiff at times with no energy. Somehow my mind and soul went back to Ute's journey. I was experiencing the other side of being unwell and it felt as if the sharing between us continued. I didn't have a community to support me, but I did have one wonderful husband and my journey had a different outcome. Stepping in to be with Ute at that time I had no idea how this would support me later on my journey.

Ute has been such a gift in my life, like a sister, a soul mate in such a short time and that has been so beautiful.

> *Ute's case was presented in a training session for health workers seven days after her death by her Clinical Physiotherapist Buffy Lee. A few excerpts below.*

Excerpt from a MND case study about Ute

UTE
09/02/2015
Buffy Lee
[Ute's] Clinical specialist physiotherapist

"I had to surrender and call social services to help me. In September 2013 I went into respite" [care].

This was Ute's quote whilst there;

'With my current stay at xxx [a rehabilitation care home] I notice the following: staff are really good and supportive both physically and emotionally, but I can't see the stars or trees and since I live in an institution I play in the league of the lovelies and sweethearts and am not taken seriously anymore. The main problem is communication: I need a reliable internet and a proper landline, a mobile doesn't work anymore given my dwindling fine motor skills and slurred speech.'

Ute's contribution to Awareness

Ute had written down her experiences from day one. This has given a unique perspective into the disease progression, and she hoped that this would be published. She used an eye-gaze system of communication from August. In October, Ute arranged an ice-bucket challenge with her friends and neighbours. She raised £300.

In mid November Ute gave a talk, via her eye gaze equipment, at an end-of-life forum. She gave an account of her disease and had good feedback.

Hospitalisation

Ute was admitted to hospital with a chest infection on Christmas eve 2014.

Her sister Zambodhi wrote;

'Thank you for all the messages of support. I am sure Ute is getting it directly. Her condition is unchanged; serious but stable for now. She is receiving maximum treatment. She was informed that she will not be intubated should further deterioration happen.

She was told that what she has is all she's got to help her through and here is what Ute wrote on her word board:

"Too early to give up!"

Whilst in hospital some difficult decisions about Ute's resuscitation status were made.

I liaised with the hospital physio as Ute would be returning home with NIPPV[54]. They also had tried a Cough Assist[55], but Ute didn't like it.

Home

Ute returned home in mid January, and I visited to see that she was coping with the NIPPV.

Her family were now around her.

She needed 24-hour care, and had fought every step of the way.

On 02/02/2015, an email from Zambodhi read,

"Ute left this life peacefully."

---

54 (NIPPV) Non Invasive Positive-Pressure Ventilation
55 A cough-assist machine helps to clear secretions

Looking back
by Zambodhi

Ute asked this question in her last letter to friends and family a few weeks before she died:

After all the losses, what is the gain?

In a conversation when she could still speak, Ute told me how tough it had been for her having to give up what she loved the most. First her husband (when she was 37 and the marriage broke down). She realised that she had a 50 percent share in the breakdown and decided to take the responsibility for her part in it. Confronting herself with some challenging aspects of her personality had a transformative effect, and as a result Ute found that more friendships were coming towards her, which she found surprising and pleasing.

Then she felt she had to let go of her daughter two or three years later (who ran away from home and didn't want to have anything to do with her for quite some time) when her daughter seemed to need support the most. Ute described how she had to build up inner trust and work with prayer, trusting that greater wisdom was at play here and praying that Franziska would be protected whilst navigating through difficult times. Later on, when they had contact again, Ute felt this time had been a 'trial of fire' and nothing could take her daughter away from the place she had for her in her heart, where she had held her throughout the struggles.

And then she had to learn a different profession because her Austrian professional farming training was not recognised in Belgium. When she had to let go of her beloved biodynamic farming, which she thought of as her life's work up to that point, a nursing training was offered to her and that became equally close to her heart. "From the cows to human beings" she commented, "this really took me a while, didn't it? And yet, nursing enriched my life so much! Look at me now, coming here [*to Stroud, England*] I got my beloved biodynamic farming back as well, with the added benefit of the CSA model of farming, isn't that amazing? This is what we were striving for in Belgium but never achieved! Giving up that which I love most has always given me something unexpected."

"Now," she continued, "there is only one more thing that I love and which will be hard to give up – and that is my life. And here I am… landed with a terminal illness! I can't think what the gift with this task might be but I have been through enough to trust and know something is going to come out of it which I cannot even imagine now."

How could she trust so much whilst facing death?

Another time when we had been talking about medical miracles, she said, referring to her illness, "I wouldn't do this properly if I didn't go all the way…"

I am asking myself the above question now. What is the gain after I lost my sister and one of my closest lifetime friends?

The last few years of her life, as difficult and challenging as they were, have become an inspiration for me: The way Ute stood by her truth, how much she wanted and welcomed the local and wider community around her, the unwavering determination to be happy whenever she could and to remain her healthy (inner) self, her amazing dedication to life in spite of tackling terminal illness and her commitment to living a meaningful of life.

By sharing her journey through NMD in this book, I also hope that caregivers, agencies, and hospitals can gain another profound human perspective on the work and collaboration among care providers. That would add further significance to Ute's life, in a manner that she would have embraced.

Above all, I hope that Ute's experiences will give rise to creativity around and enthusiasm for supporting people who are conscious but unable to communicate without assistance. I hope readers are inspired to help these individuals to express their feelings and requests.

I hope this book will inspire others as Ute inspired me.

That would be the gain.

Acknowledgements

From the time Ute received her diagnosis, support came forward. After her death, support continued to come towards me, and notably by our friend Elisabeth Demmer for the publication of this book. She approached the subject repeatedly, gently and patiently, while I was still busy recovering my own health and rebuilding my life. Her practical offers to help me were the catalyst to begin facing the task. Elisabeth invited me to her home in Luxembourg and we sat down working together intensively for one week. By the end of it we thought we would be able to publish it in German by the next spring (2020).

Later, having decided to publish the English version first, I am still experiencing support for the book, especially by my dear husband Ray, who enabled me to take the plunge and face what it takes to go all the way to publication.

Only when I got to work with Christina Bagni and Qatarina Wanders from Wandering Words, did the book finally get ready for publication. Christina, who did the first round of content editing, asked me the right questions to fill in the missing bits. As much as it was painful at times to go back to some of my memories, it also helped me to see what Ute's book needed in order to create the fuller picture she wanted. Qatarina brought her insights to the second round of content and copy editing and helped with great speed to get the work completed. Like Christina, she kept working with me on my awareness of the reader's perspective. I could not have wished for better guidance and support getting this book ready.

I like to acknowledge and thank both Ute's workplaces. They were very accommodating and prepared to accompany her in accordance with her wish to continue working as long as she could. Ute was not told to stop working, instead they adjusted the tasks for her as her health deteriorated. This left Ute free to make the decision to stop working when she was ready.

I also like to express profound gratitude for the help and support Ute received from so many professionals, first and foremost her team of carers who supported her every day. They were willing and able to learn everything Ute needed to be cared for in her own home. Such dedication to looking after her was vital to Ute's ability to get through each day, to get things done and to live her life as independently as she desired.

I like to recognise the courage of Denise, the manager of the day-care agency, who made such a difference to Ute's quality of life with her person-centred care approach, her capacity of thinking outside the box and her willingness to consider Ute's priorities and act on them. Equally important and helpful was the cooperation between day- and night-care agencies, especially towards the end of Ute's life. When Ute asked me to communicate her needs to the managers of both care agencies during her hospital stay and afterwards, they generously gave their time to me and worked things out between them, recognising my distress over Ute's suffering. They kept a calm approach and focussed solidly on supporting Ute. I feel immensely grateful that their support was so firm and that it included myself at that time of Ute's journey.

My sincere gratitude for the professional and practical support goes to the MND Society, especially for the electric wheelchair and the eye-gaze equipment without delay when she needed it. That gave Ute her mobility and her voice back, the ability to continue having a social life and study group work going on and also the ability to deal with all the issues coming up during the advanced stages of her illness and last but not least enabled her to write this book.

There is a long list of other specialists who contributed to Ute's care, including Frankie Stopford, Occupational Therapist, Buffy Lee, Clinical Specialist Physiotherapist, Katherine Broomfield and Louise Walters from the Gloucestershire Adult Speech and Language Therapy Service, the MND Specialist Nurse (at the time) Sally Hayden and Consultants in Palliative Medicine Dr Emma Husbands and Dr Cath Blinman.

With deep gratitude I want to recognise the significance of the commitment of my aunt Margarete and my late uncle Klaus, for their visits, their warm interest and for their generous financial support when we faced the need to carry on with Ute's care package during her hospital stay. Without their generous support, leading to us being able to pay for her carers privately, Ute would have been unable to communicate at all during her hospital stay. And that was the time when she needed communication most.

Furthermore, I would like to express my heartfelt gratitude to the following people for their extraordinary efforts.

Greg, who helped me on Christmas day to transport Ute's eye-gaze equipment into the hospital and to set it up in her room. It was heavy to carry, it needed the right type of extension leads and was technically beyond me at that time. Greg invited me back to his home afterwards and shared his Christmas dinner when he found out that I had not eaten anything that day.

My niece Franziska, who in the last year of her mother's life travelled across the water almost every month staying for a weekend going back to work in Germany for Monday mornings. She was a great support for her mother and me. As Ute's life drew to a close, Franziska put her life on hold and came to England for a whole month, joining me in doing everything possible to enable her mother to come home before she died. At that time care in her own home for Ute was hanging in the balance. It took both of us to support the whole situation.

Our brother Stefan, who accompanied us from his home in Switzerland and came to England as often as he could. During his visits, he was landed with practical tasks, such as repairs in and around the house, building a suitable desk so that Ute could use it when sitting in her electric wheelchair and so much more. Each time he came, the list was very long and he worked through it with the patience of an angel, often late into his last night and early in the morning of his departure. He also accompanied our mother on her visits to England, visits that otherwise would not have been possible for her.

Our friend Clare Dowling took care of the house and garden and did most creative cooking for as long as Ute could still swallow food. She made Ute's home beautiful with flowers, put Christmas and Easter decorations up and carried Ute with her presence. Clare noticed what was going on around Ute, especially as communication became increasingly difficult. When I arrived and she looked upset Ute would just spell "ask Clare".

There were many people who just helped, for example with donations to buy her buggy without giving their names. I do not know who they are. I do know about many others and am deeply touched that Ute and I received such support and that it is still active to this day with regard to Ute's book.

A feeling of being supported by the community remained, especially at the time when it became really difficult to help Ute to get some relief.

The result of all joint and individual efforts, including all those not expressly mentioned, cannot be overestimated. The last word on this has to go to Ute and I am sure she would be in agreement with interpreting the word 'carer', which she used here, in a much broader sense, encompassing everyone from whom she received support.

Finding Connection and Fulfillment in the Face of Motor Neuron Disease

> *"Without my carers I can do nothing,*
> *not even chase away a fly,*
> *with their help I can have a fulfilling life."*[56]

Photo taken by Marcus when they went out onto the fields of the farm

---

56 [from an email Nov 2014]

I am not I

I am not I.
I am the one
walking beside me whom I do not see,
whom at times I manage to visit,
and whom at other times I forget;
the one who remains silent while I talk,
the one who forgives sweetly when I hate,
the one who takes a walk when I stay inside,
the one who remains standing when I die.

Poem by Juan Ramon Jimenez

Printed in Great Britain
by Amazon